PUSHED OFF THE MOUNTAIN
SOLD DOWN THE RIVER

PUSHED OFF THE MOUNTAIN
SOLD DOWN THE RIVER

Wyoming's Search for Its Soul

Samuel Western

HOMESTEAD PUBLISHING
Moose, Wyoming
& San Francisco

I dedicate this book to my children, Sally and Cyrus, in hopes they have a chance to sing in harmony with Wyoming's song.

Acknowledgments
I would like to thank the Coe Library Staff at the University of Wyoming, Cindy Brown and everyone at the Wyoming State Archives; Helen Graham, Karen Woinoski, and Jeanne Sanchez of the Sheridan County Fulmer Library staff; the staff of the Rockpile Museum; Dick Coulter at USDA; Willie Reidel, Darla Worden; Phil Roberts; Warren Morton; Shirley Stephens; Joe Watt; Park and Mildred Fox; Stan Hathaway; T.A. Larson; Tom Gallagher; Paul Spragens; Mieke Eerkins; Wen Liu; Hans and Johanna Nel; Maryke Nel; Tex Taylor; Dick Mader; Kim and Susan Cannon; Tom Bell; Rodger Amadon; Wyoming Council on the Humanities; Ann Krielkamp; Linda Nix; Rich Lindsay; Tom Power; Richard Stroup; Shelby Gerking; M. Shahid Alam; Scott Farris, Joe Kalt; Lynton Caldwell; Jonathan Schechter and lastly the Mesa Refuge for supplying a quiet place to write.
A very special thanks to Roy Jordan and George Funk for all their assistance.

Photographic Credits
Cover photograph: Charles J. Belden "New Horizon" P,67.834, courtesy Buffalo Bill Historical Center, Cody, Wyoming.
Page 23: Woman, child and wheat, courtesy Wyoming State Archives.
Page 38: Wyoming Alfalfa, courtesy Wyoming State Archives.
Page 45: Land of Great Rewards, courtesy Wyoming State Archives.
Page 56: Ed Young's Orchard, courtesy Wyoming State Archives.
Page 101: Gebo (top), courtesy Wyoming State Archives. Jeffrey City (bottom), courtesy Mike McClure.

ISBN 0-943972-73-6
Library of Congress Control Number: 2002106486

Printed in the United States on recycled, acid free paper.
Revised edition, 2006.

7 9 10 8 6

published by
Homestead Publishing
Box 193 • Moose, Wyoming 83012
& San Francisco, CA
homesteadpublishing.net

CONTENTS

I

DON'T MESS WITH OUR MYTH

Through shimmering heat waves, Burns, Wyoming, appears in the distance like a medieval French or Italian village. Instead of castles or a fortress silhouetting the skyline, Burns presents the comfort of trees and a water tower. This city of 254 sits on a rise amidst thousands of rolling acres planted with wheat or left as pasture for cattle. Twenty miles west of the Nebraska border, it is a land of straight and gridded roads, a place where people hay their front yards.

Burns offers a type of simplicity and beauty not discussed much in the modern west. There are no grand vistas of shadowed and snow-scattered mountains, no rippling rivers or canyons so rugged and deep they awaken a new sense of wonder. Yet the landscape around Burns gives consolation. When clouds shadow sections of wheat, yet still permit—through small openings—the sun's clean rays to fall unencumbered, bearded heads dance in a shade of yellow not found on any painter's palette.

It is a transition zone: the place where the western-most edge of fecund prairie grassland meets the Rocky Mountain's foothills.

Ecologically, transition zones are exciting places. Change occurs on the periphery. Transition zones include crucibles of a social or political shift, even in distinctly staid Burns.

William H. "Willie" Riedel and his ninety-year-old mother, Effie, live four miles north of Burns on a 480-acre homestead complete with the usual assortment of machinery and scattered outbuildings. Chinese elm and lilacs offer shade. Willie's mother, a widow, lives in a shingled house with a weathervane stuck permanently on south-west. The house gently resonates with the sound of bees; a hive resides in the east wall of the building. They've existed in peaceful cohabitation with the Riedels for decades.

Cooking before a gas stove she bought in 1952, Effie talks about homesteading. Her father originally patented a different piece of land, located five miles away, in 1909. Effie was born two years following. In her youth, chores kept her occupied. "We had 300 chickens. The eggs paid for the groceries," she said. "We'd bring them up to the store and they'd buy them. We milked cows and my mother churned the butter; we sold it in one pound blocks."

Safeways or Albertsons hold little appeal to Effie. "I haven't been to the grocery store in Lord knows how many years," she said. She and Willie, she calls him "William," butcher a calf each year. Simple food and a simple way of life have been her companions. She's lived on her current property since 1940. "Me and my husband raised seven kids and paid for the farm. My father gave me the wheat crop for a wedding present."

Riedel lives in a trailer 100 yards south of the house. He is a bachelor and a classic small Wyoming rancher. He runs seventy head of cattle and grows wheat, hay, and occasionally oats for feed. Yet unlike most Wyoming ranchers, Riedel does not count on outside income to supplement the bounty of his land. He has no hired hand. Although the state of Wyoming would like to think otherwise—it boasts 9,200 ranchers and farmers—there are only a handful of truly independent operators like Riedel.

He also is an agent provocateur, an odd distinction in that Riedel is a bullnecked affable man with a belly laugh who likes to get along with everyone. He's a local boy who exemplifies the rancher ethic of economy. The 4,000 bushels of wheat he raises annually sells cheap, but he manages to make a modest profit, mostly by avoiding monthly machinery payments. "I don't go out and buy these big, fancy tractors." Once, in a fit of profligacy, he purchased a new manure spreader. "It ought to last me as long as I'll ever need one," he said.

Still, he laments, "at $2.50 per bushel, it's hard to make money," echoing the hard times most wheat growers suffer nationwide.

One would think this small rancher's willingness to endure would build solidarity with fellow producers. Yet Riedel has found himself ostracized because he broke an ironclad Wyoming code: don't question the rules for obtaining a state grazing lease.

When Wyoming entered the union in 1890, it accepted township sections sixteen and thirty-six from the federal government for "support of the common schools," as Wyoming Act of Admission reads. Wyoming leases most of its 3.4 million acres of land. Grazing leases usually expire every ten years.

However, through a curious blend of protective politics, the state owns the roughly 4,000 grazing properties in title only. In reality, these parcels of land are *de facto* personal property of the lessees. State law prevents competitive bidding. When a lease expires, anyone wishing to bid on the lease may give one bid and one bid only, with the current lessee given the right to top that one bid. No counter bidding allowed. This system permits leases to be handed down generation to generation within one family without ever having to give up the lease, then rebid for it.

In 1998, Riedel filed a lawsuit after he'd lost a bid to lease a 640-acre piece of state ground in section thirty-six, township sixteen, range sixty-three in Laramie County. As the crow flies, the section is about two miles from the Riedel homestead. Even though Riedel submitted a $6,000 bid for the lease, the state board of land commissioners gave the lease to Craig Andersen, a school teacher and the current leaseholder, who bid $4,538. As long as Andersen matched Riedel's bid within fifteen days, which he did, Wyoming's preferential bid system all but guarantees Andersen's retention of the lease.

Riedel went to court demanding, among other things, that the preferential bid system be abandoned. "It's a rip-off, these state land lease deals. Some of these parcels have been with a family for so dang long they think they own it," Riedel said.

Thus far, his case in court hasn't progressed far. In November 2001, he lost at the district court level, but says he will appeal. In the big picture, however, Riedel's case represents troubles far more deep than convoluted leasing law or even economics. Riedel recognizes this and plainly puts into words what many feel, but speak about reluctantly. "Wyoming wants to go ahead but they want to stay back one hundred years, the way it seems. They don't want change."

"Who doesn't want change?" I ask.

"The government," says Riedel. "It's been working, so why change it, that's the way they look at it. But hey, times is changing."

The inferred message of Riedel's statement begs an obvious question: If the state hangs on to the past, how can it deny a person who lives out Wyoming's deepest mythology, the small independent rancher, the right to a grazing lease on state land? What does that say about Wyoming's priorities?

Wyoming's priorities, I discovered, defy easy explanation. A stranger driving through the state might make note of Wyoming's fine roads, its modern schools, its massive coal mines and productive gas fields. Furthermore, such assets might reasonably lead a stranger to a sunny assessment about Wyoming's future. In April 2001, Sung Won Sohn, a former presidential advisor from the San Francisco-based Wells Fargo bank, stood before an audience in Casper and said just that. "The economic outlook in Wyoming looks very good," he said.

Dr. Sohn's statement carries the assumption that natural resources bring wealth. They can, but it's a strange and slippery richness that often leads not to prosperity, but insolvency. Since territorial days, Wyoming has bet on cattle, oil, coal, and gas to bring the state abundance. The gamble has failed. Out of 112 years of existence, probably only forty were not lean. The state's history is one of poverty punctuated by sporadic prosperity: 1903-1919, 1940-1945, and the energy decade created by the Arab oil embargo, approximately 1973-1983. The 1950s and 1960s also had isolated years of abundance, when uranium was booming, for example.

Since the Depression, Wyoming has stood where Ireland remained for centuries: a poor, friendly, hard-working state that exports everything, especially talent. The state leaks brain power like thin tea through a colander. Depending on whose figures you believe, 50-75 percent of all college graduates in Wyoming leave the state looking for work.

Collectively Wyoming struggles with the idea that people and their ideas, not natural resources, bring wealth. The state persistently elects leaders who feel if they build one more dam, punch another logging road in a National Forest, cut agriculture another check, or give oil and gas producers an additional tax break, then prosperity will arrive.

No governor in Wyoming's history has publicly acknowledged, for example, that the state's agricultural policy, which gives more financial aid to ranchers than does any other state in the union, would cause coronary arrest in the most sympathetic farm-cost analyst. The policy has cost Wyoming hundreds of millions, probably billions, of dollars over the years. No leader can admit that agriculture has broken up more families and chased more people out of the state than any other single industry. No figurehead has even publicly admitted something so simple, so unequivocally true, that Wyoming is a marginal agricultural state. It produces less than 2 percent of the total value of America's cattle and calves.

With few exceptions, Wyoming leaders promote commodity production as a path to wealth, despite glaring evidence to the contrary. For example, in 1968, after the United States had enjoyed one of the longest economic expansions of the twentieth century, then-Governor Stanley K. Hathaway discovered that Wyoming had $80.00 in the state's general fund. The larder was empty. How could one of the leading energy states in the nation be so poor? The predicament is all the more puzzling because it was the second time in 35 years that the state found itself flat broke.

Furthermore, if not for payments from the federal government, oil and gas severance tax, and prodigious sums squirreled away during a decade of high energy prices (1973-1983), Wyoming would have again found itself in dire financial straits by the late 1980s. The greatest economic expansion in U.S. history, 1992-2001, stopped cold at the Wyoming border.

Lastly, Wyoming voters elect leaders who harbor and project a fantasy of the state's history—one of rugged independence. If independence is defined as self-sufficiency, i.e., the ability to generate enough income to keep a healthy economy with minimal outside influence, then Wyoming has fallen profoundly short of the goal. Leaders promote a portrait of a wild, free land where everyone's a trapper, homesteader, bronco rider, wildcatter, do-or-die prospector, or, the most persistent image: cattle baron. In fact, the number of salaried working men and women: coal miner, railroad worker, laundress, cowboy, government surveyor, tie hack, schoolteacher, or town clerk always outnumbered Wyoming's ranch-owning residents.

Little has changed. As of 2002, the largest private sector

employer in Wyoming is the Wal-Mart Corporation of Bentonville, Arkansas. This labor-based history bothers the state tremendously. It is as if it's ashamed of working for a wage. Yet sweeping history under the rug creates a warped self-image. "Our traditions are behind us," noted classical scholar Michael Grant, "whether we like it or not. If we remain unconscious of our traditions, we are their victims all the same."

An economist I interviewed regarding Wyoming's financial plight emphasized this point: "Look, if you're not prepared to face the past, how can you possibly face the future? Wyoming just can't face its past."

After writing about the West for almost 20 years, I decided to see if I could discover why Wyoming chose to bury or ignore certain elements of its history. About midway through this project, after months spent reading, researching, and interviewing, I realized Wyoming is searching for its soul. In earthly terms, it means Wyoming wants—desperately, almost secretly—an inner identity not defined or controlled by outside terms.

Wyoming does not enjoy immunity from outside forces. No state does. But since territorial times, Wyoming has seethed at its impotence in Washington. And instead of community, the state ended up with transient workers and a constant out-migration of beings who, short of enduring abject poverty, would do anything to stay in the state. Stan Hathaway put it succinctly: "There is no better place in the world to feel satisfaction than in the state of Wyoming—if you can make a good living."

People in Wyoming generally don't worry about making too much money. Open space, safe neighborhoods, physical beauty, lack of congestion, clean air and great recreational opportunities keep people living in Wyoming. For generations, however, Wyoming residents issued a plea: give us an economy that permits our children to stay here and work, give us a federal government that trusts that we can make good decisions on our own, give us a community that won't explode at the high price of oil then sink into charred embers as demand drops.

Wyoming's burly mythology of independence, however, directly contradicts the idea of community. The empirical evidence concerning employment, migration, and revenue starkly reveals that

Wyoming's current interpretation of the homestead/ranching/wild-catter myth is a community killer extraordinaire. The state seems primed for *perestroika*, the Russian term for political and economic reform. Still, people like Willie Riedel have discovered that the state's mythology of independence has created an extraordinary vaccine against modification.

In a seminal article published in the *Annals of Wyoming*, historian Roy Jordan wrote, "romantic history is dangerous history. The myth of innocent pioneering has left a false impression of the uniqueness of our [Wyoming's] history; that 'frontier' myth has been stressed so long as to make the state colorful, but it also causes it to be irrelevant at the same time."

Then Jordan, in one sentence, encapsulated Wyoming's mythological struggle. "In politics, as in a culture, it is not what you in fact favor or hinder, it is what you appear to champion or obstruct. That is how mythologies and lifestyles are created and sustained."

Here is an example of how this works. In 1999, State Senator Jim Twiford, reportedly under pressure from his ranching constituents, threatened to strip funding from the University of Wyoming Law School after professor Debra Donahue wrote a book that challenged grazing permits on arid federal land.

"I know these professors have academic freedom, but we've got some unlicensed, unbridled folks running over there that ought to be smarter than to be biting the hand that's feeding them," Twiford told the *Casper Star-Tribune*. Twiford admitted that he hadn't yet read Donahue's book, *The Western Range Revisited: Removing Livestock from Public Lands to Conserve Native Biodiversity*, but that ranchers in his area objected to the very idea of its publication. "I have all of the ranching community calling me, saying, 'Why in the hell should we support an institution that is out to change the culture of Wyoming, and, in essence, part of the tax base that's going to feed that university so she has a job? She's out to destroy us with her book.'"

Senator Twiford did not, in the end, introduce any such legislation. The implied message of such political threat could not have been clearer, however. It signaled an imperial intolerance towards new and possibly painful ideas. But to paraphrase Alexander Hamilton in the *Federalist Papers*, "heresies can rarely be cured by prosecution."

It is remarkable that the president of the Wyoming Senate believed that agriculture remained a critical part of the state's economy. The discouraging data documenting the industry's decline since 1919 has been available for decades. Agriculture in Wyoming is largely a ceremonial occupation.

Most proponents of agriculture say they're trying to protect their lifestyle or way of life. What "way of life" promotes economic dependency and, most importantly, bleeds a state of its youth and vitality?

The 2000 US Census spelled out the grim details of promoting a Wyoming way of life. Eleven Wyoming counties, five of them leaders in agriculture, suffered population loss between 1990-2000. Carbon County, the third largest producer of livestock and crops in the state, led the exodus with a 6.1 percent decrease in population from 1990-2000.

Not surprisingly, these counties find themselves in tough economic times and unable to pay for local services, primarily schooling. The leading agricultural county in Wyoming, Goshen, produces fifteen percent of Wyoming's agricultural value. Goshen county also is among the most dependent upon relying on state and federal sources for local needs.

Gray hair is common not only in these counties, but all over the state. "During the last twenty years, Wyoming has aged faster than any other state in the country," said Jonathan Schechter of the Charture Institute of Jackson. Schecter spent months analyzing the 2000 Census. "For the first time in the state's history, there are more people thirty-five and older than there are thirty-four and younger. All of our (population) growth in the 1990s came from those thirty-five and older. We actually had a decrease among those who are thirty-four or younger."

It's a double whammy, a two-generational void, according to Schechter. "Not only do you have fewer kids, but you also are wiping out the generation that produces children. We don't have the twenty to thirty-four year-old generation making babies. We are in a demographic death spiral."

This is not an argument against agriculture (the science and art of growing food) or stewardship practiced by Wyoming ranchers. Nor is it a recommendation to scuttle the hopes of Future Farmers of

America or 4-H. The objection is to *agriculturalism,* a "way-of-life" mindset with an intrinsic sense of superiority to all other professions and an entrenched sense of entitlement, specifically expecting financial and political protection. Wyoming's farmers and ranchers project an image that they are descendents of Jefferson's agrarian republic and that on their survival rests the economic health of Wyoming.

Most ranchers privately concede that Wyoming agriculture has been in deep trouble for generations. Some make dire public admissions. "Our breed is dying," wrote Jack Turnell in an editorial in *Cow Country,* the journal of the Wyoming Stock Growers Association, "we must pull together." Yet the minute someone publicly concludes that agriculture plays only a minor part in Wyoming's economy, ranching interests sound the claxon. In fact, Wyoming ranchers and farmers tolerate little criticism of their industry. "Don't Mess with Our Myth" might be the credo of Wyoming agriculture.

At the core, at the very heart of Wyoming's community woes, beyond its struggle with the federal government and fights over energy taxation is a state that wanted Jefferson's children—small farmers—but could not manage to attract them. The story of Wyoming homesteaders is one of heartbreak and, for the majority of ranching aspirants, failure.

Wyoming struggles with this unromantic view of history and understandably so, for the homesteader image fulfills every sacred iconographic need for those yearning for community: family, working the land, stewardship, continuity, independence, and, most critically, feeding the nation's hungry. For a state struggling with the idea of community, the wound of the failed homesteader and small farmer remains too painful to examine.

The homesteader tragedy of the Dakotas and Montana did not significantly differ from that of Wyoming. But the attitude towards, and response to, the Depression partially explain the discrepancy between Wyoming and the rest of the West. Most states accept that the Depression flattened the homesteader and dramatically changed the very nature of American agriculture. The Wyoming version, however, claims homesteaders settled the territory, toughed out the Depression, and went on to form the moral and economic backbone of the state.

The story stuck, despite historical evidence to the contrary. When the homesteader myth spliced with the cowboy mystique, the fusion wielded ungodly power. This is true even though the homesteader and the cowboy were often from different cuts of cloth and not infrequently at odds with each other. The writer Wallace Stegner gave up on the mythic cowboy, even though the figure irritated him all his life. "I would obviously like to bury him," he confessed in *The American West as Living Space*. "But I know I can't. He's a faster gun than I am."

While Stegner found the cowboy myth obnoxious and impregnable, the homesteader legend presented problems. Stegner's family homesteaded on the Saskatchewan-Montana border. The enterprise met a typical demise: it failed and the land was returned to the provincial (or federal, in the case of U.S. land) government and put back into range. Stegner refused to return to his homestead as an adult. "I don't want to find, as I know I will if I go down there, that we have vanished without a trace like a boat sunk in mid-ocean," he said in his autobiographical *Wolf Willow*. "I don't want our shack to be gone, as I know it is."

But importantly, Stegner does not glorify the homesteader, enshrining him or her, but instead agrees to an uneasy truce with his fear of being forgotten. "To go down there armed with only a memory and find every trace of our passage wiped away–that would be to reduce my family, myself, the hard effort of years to solipsism, to make us as fictive as a dream."

As the years passed in Wyoming, the defenders of the homesteader/cowboy/small rancher myth joined with a force who wasn't quite their enemy, but was no friend, either: the large stockmen. Ranchers, not just in Wyoming but all over the West, especially in the 1880s and 1890s, fought with spur and bullet to prevent homesteaders from staking the open range.

Most federal land intended for individual homesteaders ended up as an addition to a stockman's spread or was returned to the Bureau of Land Management. This detail did not seem to send a quiver down the foundation of the homesteader/rancher ideology. Surviving required help from the government. The source, at first, was Washington, which gave away the land itself, irrigation water, and cheap grazing. But Wyoming got into the act by loaning money to ranchers and farmers. In 1915, voters amended the Wyoming Constitution, giving stockmen the exclusive right to borrow money from the state's common school fund. The amended Constitution thus protected Wyoming agriculture from having to compete with other businesses for capital.

Despite such a shield, arid farming and grazing in Wyoming came perilously close to expiring in the early 1930s. Ironically, sheep numbers went to all-time highs. Farmers planted record acres of crops. They still went under. The Depression and drought, in fact, hammered Wyoming. But destitution inured Wyomingites to an extraordinary hardness and ability to endure suffering. Works Progress Administration employee Loreena Hickok, sent by her boss Harry Hopkins to survey how Wyoming was faring in the Depression, wrote Hopkins on September 8th, 1934, that "conditions were as bad as the Dakotas, but people don't complain. They have an awful sense of patience."

Organizations associated with cattle fell. In 1930, the Wyoming Stock Growers Association found itself with $565 in its bank account. In 1936, workers tore down the famed Cheyenne Club, ironically to make room for a chamber of commerce building. Demand for beef and cattle plummeted to an all-time low.

If left alone to settle to an unfettered level of economic importance, agriculture would have faded into obscurity. But state leaders didn't let that happen. Even though the state was half a million dollars in debt, then-Governor Frank Emerson tried in 1928 to add an additional $1 million to the Farm Loan Board Revolving Fund. Then, in 1935, an important act for enshrining the cowboy myth: the bucking bronco was affixed on the license plate. This symbol made Wyoming's association with agriculture an obligation, not a choice.

I'm getting ahead of my story. But one more facet of the tale needs to be mentioned. After World War Two, record numbers of American youth left agriculture. Ranch income plunged. This didn't seem to faze the Wyoming myth. If anything, it thrived and was joined by a very odd character. Under the guise of the rugged independent miner or wildcatter, Wyoming's oil and gas interests joined the homesteader/cowboy alliance. This latest addition gave the movement what it desperately needed: money.

Money, mystique, and myth—a formidable triumvirate and effective tool for keeping competing ideas at bay. The problem is that different and opposing ideas make a society whole. The seal of the United States declares: *e pluribus unum*, (out of many, one), the Latin term for the word "pluralism." This nation can tolerate many beliefs: that is one of its civic strengths. Pluralism rejects putting stock solely in one system or demonizing someone who doesn't think along accepted lines. It embraces the necessity of trade-offs, including concessions that go against the grain. It is an essential ingredient in the concept of community.

A way-of-life mythology has, ironically, stripped Wyoming of life-giving vigor. When commodity prices are good, this mythology lets Wyoming see the world from a mountaintop. Then prices drop and the mythology pushes Wyoming off a granite peak. Its dreams get sold down the river. This rendition of mythology has left Wyoming dependent on federal largess, bankrupt but for a veneer of oil and gas money, and, for sixty years, feeling helpless as it watches its young leave. Since territorial times, the mythology has left Wyoming open to opportunists of all persuasions.

The Italian novelist Iganzio Silone commented that "revolutions, like trees, should be judged by their fruit." The same standard can be applied to a state's public policy. Despite lots of money, billions of dollars in fact, from oil, gas, and coal revenues over the last thirty years, Wyoming still suffers. Wyoming myths promise *freedom* to residents and corporations. But if this credo of liberty works, how can Wyoming find itself near the bottom of the economic pile?

The state that boasts the ultimate pro-business stance—no income or corporate tax, loose labor laws, and millions in agriculture subsidies—cannot keep its own children. It finds itself embarrassingly dependent on the federal government. Like any welfare recipient, it sees, by necessity, any job as a good job. How did Wyoming get into this position in the first place? And what makes the state so reluctant to face its past? Finding out requires a foray into the inscrutable mind of Ulysses S. Grant.

II

ALMOST STILL BORN

President Ulysses S. Grant was not a man of great charisma or cerebral endeavors. As E. B. Long, a onetime professor of history at the University of Wyoming noted, Grant "was not an intellectual; he was not a man of culture. He was a bourgeois man." These aspersions didn't hinder his steadiness, courage, and conviction, as his military record clearly revealed.

As a holder of middle-class values, Grant embraced what he knew and what had helped him succeed. He liked men with Union army backgrounds and he liked loyalty. Many an appointee found himself jobless because Grant suspected him of even mild perfidy. Repeatedly, this matter of loyalty surfaced in Grant's political career; it reveals one of the president's more enigmatic shortcomings: he had a hard time choosing men who would be loyal. In short, Grant had trouble judging character.

His appointees for Wyoming Territory were a case in point. Wyoming had been a personnel nightmare for the president since its inception as a territory in 1868. Two appointees, Territorial Secretary Edward M. Lee and U.S. Marshall Church Howe, had been involved in a feud over a territorial printing contract. Yet accusations circled not around the issue of who got to print legislative proceedings and session laws, but on personal misconduct. Lee, said Howe, "has been beastly drunk... and has been living publicly with a notorious prostitute." Grant fired Lee.

Then some of Lee's supporters began writing Grant detailing Howe's abuse of the public trust. They claimed Howe failed to pay jurors and the expenses of the court, even though he had received money from the Treasury for that express purpose. Grant fired Howe, but recanted when Howe's replacement, Robert Milroy, lasted only a few days in Cheyenne.

Milroy, a financially troubled former Union army general, took the job in Cheyenne not for adventure, party loyalty, or the chance to be part of building a new territory, but financial gain. "I frankly admit that the emoluments constitute the inducement for my seeking an appointment," he wrote to Grant. Within three days after arriving in Cheyenne, Milroy discovered that his expected salary of $1,000 per annum would not materialize and he left under the cover of darkness on a cattle train.

Howe and his followers then pointed out the greed of another Grant appointee, Frank Wolcott. As a receiver in the United States Land Office, Wolcott had illegally staked land in the Iron Mountain country. Aware of the plans for a railroad to exploit the region's supposed iron-ore wealth, Wolcott wanted to benefit financially. Grant fired Wolcott. This irritated then-governor John Campbell, who seemed miffed at the influence of his enemy Howe. Campbell wrote to Grant saying that Howe had travelled east, leaving his and the territory's business in disarray. This was an audacious complaint from Campbell, a man who had taken over 250 days of personal leave between December 1869 and December 1872. For a second time, Grant fired Howe, only to replace him with the arrant claim jumper, Frank Wolcott.

Now Grant faced more personnel woes. Governor Campbell had written Grant complaining that two more of his appointees, the Surveyor General Silas Reed and the new Territorial Secretary Herman Glafcke, were guilty of anti-Grant activities within the Republican Party. Grant, who was sensitive about what people said of him, would eventually fire them both. But with typical Grant vacillation, he'd hire them back, Reed to his original position and Glafcke as postmaster of Cheyenne.

Grant was ready to jettison Wyoming. On December 17, 1872, Grant told the House Committee on Territories that Wyoming should be dissolved. "Wyoming would never obtain the necessary population to make it a state," he said. As such "it was a useless expense and burden to keep up a Territorial form of government," he said.

"Let Colorado, Utah, Montana, and Idaho divide the area among them," he concluded.

Population concerns aside, Wyoming probably exceeded Grant's tolerance for mixing of business and government. Later in his presidency, Grant got into trouble for his solicitous attitude towards special interests. But he had limits. He signed legislation in 1871 curbing railroad land grants for just that reason. While commercialism and blatant catering to speculators were normal in western settlement, no territory had sunk as low as Wyoming. It had been formed for a purpose and one purpose only: advancing the cause of the Union Pacific Railroad. John Campbell had made this plain in his first speech to Wyoming's nascent legislative assembly.

"For the first time in the history of our country the organization of a Territorial government was rendered necessary by the building of a railroad.... It is our duty to shape our action in all the departments of the Territorial government so as to assist in carrying out the object to which the Government and the proprietors and builders of the road had in view."

Although Grant had just two months previously signed legislation establishing Yellowstone National Park, thus protecting it from miners and cattlemen, the president was not known as a dewy-eyed preservationist. Grant, in fact, liked development. But he felt political favor should be reserved not to corporations, but to the individual homesteader. "The remarkable growth and prosperity of our new States and Territories," he said in his 1870 annual address to Congress, "attest to the wisdom of the legislature which invites the tiller of the soil to secure a permanent home on terms within the reach of all. The pioneer who incurs the dangers and privations of a frontier life, and thus aids in laying the foundation of new commonwealths, renders a signal service to his country, and is entitled to special favor and protection."

The problem was Wyoming couldn't attract farmers, a critical development for a new territory. With the ink on Wyoming's territorial charter just three years old, Grant wondered how this land would survive. Those knowledgeable about this new territory were betting against it. "Cheyenne cannot hope for a permanency until the surrounding country is settled by a thriving farming population," wrote Ferdinand Hayden, head of the United States Geological

Survey on the Territories. In 1870, he noted that while Nebraska had 647,031 acres under cultivation and Colorado 95,594, Wyoming had only 338 acres of plowed farmland in the entire state.

This lack of arable land worried James Ashford, a congressman from Ohio and head of the powerful Committee on the Territories, that he eventually recommended against territory status. He referred to the drive for Wyoming Territory as "a scheme for officeholders."

"There was not fertility in the soil to subsist a population sufficient for a single congressional district," said Ashford. "Not one acre in a thousand can be irrigated."

Besides fretting about poor land and a lack of farmers, Grant probably worried about Wyoming's shortage of precious minerals. South Pass City, a lode of purported promise discovered in 1867, turned out to be a disappointment. In all it produced about $2 million worth of gold. By comparison, Montana mines produced $16 million in 1867 alone and kept on bearing for another century.

Miners were self-contained entrepreneurs. They needed no government subsidy to induce their industry. Rather they simply flocked to gold and silver ore bodies. Often they went where they weren't wanted, such as Indian land, which met with Grant's disapprobation. But more importantly, hard-rock miners had given states surrounding Wyoming an almost instant source of capital. Exploiting a coal mine or oil field usually necessitated a substantial capital outlay and ready markets. Gold and silver mining merely required determination, a mule and a sluice pan. Easily transportable, dust or nugget could be sold anywhere. This readily conveyed, uniform measure of wealth was a universal currency in the West, especially in remote areas. States like Wyoming without dust or nugget suffered from a lack of entrepreneurs.

Lastly, Wyoming territory's raison d'être, the Union Pacific Rail Road, had just lost its monopoly. The completion of the Kansas Pacific and Denver Pacific railroads in 1871 made Denver no longer dependent on Cheyenne for goods, a serious economic blow to Wyoming merchants.

In the end, however, Congress declined to dismantle the new quadrangle of land. The Colorado statehood bill had numerous manifestations. In December of 1873, the House Committee on Territories shelved the version that favored snipping up Wyoming. But the

Woman, child and wheat: This photo, taken around Newcastle in 1915, symbolizes what eluded Wyoming: family, food and fertile land.

10,000 or so citizens of Wyoming, most of them living around Cheyenne or Laramie, sensed Washington's unease. A not-so-quiet sensation, one that derives from being overly dependent on someone, began to infect the territory. The state feared for its very survival.

What saved the territory was a lanky cow driven up from south of the Red River–the Texas Longhorn. A series of mild winters convinced cattlemen that stock could be left to graze all winter without supplemental feeding. The 1869 Wyoming General Laws state that "cattle and all kinds of stock can be fattened without being housed or foddered in winter time. With these extraordinary facilities, Wyoming can successfully compete with all the world in the matter of stock growing, and upon her plains there is room and sustenance for millions of cattle and unnumbered herds of wool-bearing animals."

Fortified by military contracts for beef and the need to feed crews laying down Union Pacific track, cattlemen began enlarging

herds in southern Wyoming. Assessment rolls in 1870 for Wyoming
Territory show 8,143 cattle on record. By 1885, cattle numbers exceeded one million.

Using Cheyenne as their administrative center, cattlemen gave
Wyoming purpose; it could be said without exaggeration that cattle
saved the state of Wyoming from dissection and oblivion. A 1908
Wyoming Department of Immigration pamphlet headlined the is-
sue succinctly: "The Cattleman and His Range Made the State of
Wyoming Possible."

But in Wyoming's haste to embrace those who gave it standing,
it cast a haunting legacy: a dependency on outside capital, an incli-
nation to embrace large corporations that depend on natural resources, and, probably most importantly, a profound prejudice towards entrepreneurs. The cattle boom, while romantic and, for a
few, highly remunerative, was short-lived and ultimately destruc-
tive to Wyoming.

I'm not referring to any ecological damage that occurred due
to overgrazing; the detriment was philosophical and economic.
Wyoming's bovine-based prosperity wasn't so much a cattle boom
as it was a remarkable chapter in commodity administration. About
fifty or so wealthy individuals held sway in what was then the political epicenter of the territory: Cheyenne.

"With the territorial capital, the largest block of votes, the most
wealth, the most skilled politicians, Laramie County dominated
politics well into the statehood era," said Lewis Gould in his doc-
toral thesis on Willis Van DeVanter, a Supreme Court Justice who
cut his teeth on Wyoming law and politics. The historian Gilbert
Stelter, who specializes in the urban development of the frontier
West, wrote that Cheyenne "never became a characteristic cow town
like Dodge City, Kansas, or Miles City, Montana, for it did not become a rendezvous for driver and herders, the colorful cowboys of
the cattle West. Rather, Cheyenne served as the residence and administration headquarters of the emerging cattle kings."

But this power eventually came at the state's expense, for the
upswing permitted Wyoming to skip a critical stage that so worried
Grant: the era of the small farmer. Gould commented that "no other
part of the arid region had such a glaring lack of an agricultural
base; even the desert state of Nevada had five times as many people

engaged in crop agriculture as Wyoming in 1870. Since a strong agricultural sector was necessary for a viable society or stable economy, the territory began with a crushing handicap."

Throughout history, a region's economic well-being depended on small farmers. Living as they did in isolated areas, farmers perforce became millwrights to grind their grain. They fussed and tinkered with gears, water pressure, and other items mechanical. They wanted better plows, more efficient power sources before the plow, better looms for their wool, more consistent energy sources to looms and grinding wheels for their corn; they wanted better uses for their crops; they formed cooperatives to get higher prices; they advocated cheaper ways to get produce to market.

Conversely, ranchers took a passive and solitary approach against their calling. "Unlike the farmer, his financial rewards were greatest when his isolation was the most complete," wrote Ernest Osgood in *The Day of the Cattleman*. Ranchers waited for rain and warm weather to provide grass. Other than to provide rudimentary improvements, Wyoming ranchers—especially in the early days—saw no financial reason to wrestle with mother nature. Their calling was aristocratic to its core: vast plains that supported limitless cattle, untended, needing no labor, and therefore an occupation fit for a gentleman. In his 1878 Report to the Secretary of the Interior, Governor John Hoyt called cows and grass "pastoral resources." Pastoral means the earth will provide unattended.

The proactive stance of farmers, by contrast, with the land—to clear, level, drain, plow, harrow, irrigate (plus harvest, store, and market crops)—required an entrepreneurial bent. They invented new machinery, as the Englishman Patrick Bell did with the first reaping machine. If not tinkerers and entrepreneurs themselves, tillers of the soil provided material to those who are, as did the farmers of Grand Detour, Illinois, with a young inventive blacksmith named John Deere.

Moreover, societies that base their pride and economy on large landholders rarely take kindly to merchants. Entrepreneurs and shopkeepers are snubbed. "If we learn anything from the history of economic development, it is that culture makes all the difference," says historian David Landes. So prevalent is this anti-commerce theme in pastoral economies that the first acquisition a wealthy entrepreneur makes with newly earned money is a ranch or farm, thus giving himself legitimacy. It's analogous to the newly wealthy in Europe buying a title.

This reverential attitude towards large landholders leads to core impoverishment. The current manifestation of this veneration in Wyoming is the subsidies it gives agriculture: low rents for grazing fees, below-cost loans, government-funded irrigation, and a host of tax exemptions. Supporters of such programs usually tout the benefits of steady jobs and the multiplier effect. Rarely mentioned is that historically pastoral or grazing economies can't—or won't—tolerate many taxes.

"In Wyoming territory, the chief form of taxable property was cattle," wrote historian William Neil, "but many ranchers were escaping the payment of proper taxes on their herds by seeing they were grossly undervalued or not valued at all."

You can hear the consternation in Governor John Hoyt's voice as he wrestled with his perception of cattlemen, whom he considered upright, versus what he saw they were doing to Wyoming's treasury. "The discrepancy [which he termed as large] between returned and real numbers [of cattle] requires to be explained upon the grounds that it will acquit owners of attempts to defraud the treasury, for the returns are sworn to by as honorable and upright class of men as can be found in any community of the world."

In 1933, when cattlemen paid the highest proportion of Wyoming's assessed valuation, about 42 percent, the state was broke. And, according to then-Governor Leslie Miller, it had been in the red for years. Throughout Wyoming's history, agriculture struggled mightily to pay the bills. Oftentimes ranchers couldn't, denying the state critical funding to build infrastructure. This increasingly put the onus on someone else, like the federal government, to pay the bills. For example, in 1931, there were only 351 miles of paved or oiled roads in Wyoming. By 1939, it had 3,400 miles of them, courtesy not of the local tax base, but of Washington.

The cattle era set a recalcitrant pattern of boom and bust for Wyoming. This cycle efficiently retains wealth among just a few. The wealthy have enough set aside to survive. In the bust, they buy, and await the next boom or upswing in prices. However, a bust deals the entrepreneur, who often borrowed heavily, a severe blow. Only the most determined can pick up the pieces and re-build.

The man who almost scuttled Wyoming, Ulysses Grant, died in 1885, eaten away by throat cancer. His papers give scant indication that he devoted much thought to the western territories. His *Memoirs*, penned in the last year of his life, skipped the eight years of his presidency altogether. He did, however, salute the West as a place that gave Americans more breathing room.

In 1885, Wyoming was at the height of its economic power, but was about to step off a financial cliff with the fall of cattle prices in 1887, a tumble from which it has never fully recovered.

III

CALEDONIAN PIT BULL

B lood sports gave Wyoming governor Thomas Moonlight plea-
sure. After taking office in 1887, he held cockfights behind the
executive mansion in Cheyenne, much to his wife's disapproval.
The governor attended prizefights. Pigeon shoots so captured his
attention that he would buy the birds literally by the wagonload,
then take on challengers. He didn't miss often; during his tenure in
office, Moonlight purportedly beat the world champion wing shot.

Yet Moonlight's Victorian sense of decorum and justice ruled
his realm with a stern hand. He disapproved of saloons and cigar
stores operating on Sundays. Vigilantism found no sympathy when
Moonlight held the executive office. Moonlight's 1888 address to
the Wyoming legislature ended rather abruptly with a paraphrase
of Abraham Lincoln's famous words from his second inaugural address, "charity for all and malice towards none."

This magnanimity did not extend, however, to those who trans-
gressed on Moonlight's sense of justice. In 1865, as an army officer
stationed at Fort Laramie, Moonlight hanged two Sioux warriors up
by their necks with chains, letting them choke to death.

Neither did his compassion bestow understanding to the intri-
cacies of large-scale ranches. Appointed governor to Wyoming Territory by Grover Cleveland, Moonlight came face-to-face with the
power and opposition of the Wyoming cattle industry. Moonlight
was a Scottish-born granger. Stout, dogmatic, and stubborn, he cru-
saded for homesteaders. In Wyoming, this meant advancing the
cause of small farms at the expense of infuriating big landowners.

Moonlight came to Wyoming at the cusp of change. The bitter winter of 1886-1887 proved to be one of the most formidable in Wyoming's recorded history. The cattle companies, already staggering from overstocking and plummeting prices, folded as a result of the heavy snow and cold. Some ranches lost up to 80 percent of their herd. The Cheyenne Club closed its doors. Wyoming's economy collapsed. "It was utter ruin," wrote John Clay of Cheyenne in 1887. "Not only the banks made a total loss, but the employees down to the hired girl saw their savings disappear."

This breakdown, thought Moonlight, was a perfect time to alter Wyoming's economic engine. He reasoned that the financially strapped ranches would break up, leading to an immigration of farmers who "would put their hands on the plow and not look back."

His travels around Wyoming told Moonlight that ranching practices had to change. In 1888, Moonlight wrote Joel Harris of Rutland, Vermont, "I do not believe the cattle business or horse business can be made to pay in Wyoming when there must be six months of feeding, except by the small holder in conjunction with agriculture. I traveled over 2000 miles in a buggy during the summers of 1887 and 1888 for the purpose of seeing and am convinced of what I say. Many of the ranges have been fed to death (*grasses so short that they can't recover*) and animals are stunted and runty, thereby bring[ing] lower prices. The cattle business has been overdone in all the range country and the result is half-fed small cattle which have limited market and a limited price. The good cattle will bring a good price, but the difficulty is to make them good."

While the "white disaster," as cattlemen called the winter of 1886-1887, culled stockmen from the range, the 1890 Census shows Wyoming was short on farmers. While a highly industrious irrigation scheme helped agriculture, next to Rhode Island, no state had as few improved acres as Wyoming: 476, 831. By contrast, Nebraska had fifteen million. When it came to small truck farms–those with fewer than fifty acres–Wyoming was last in the nation with thirty. It was the poorest in manufacturing, with only 190 businesses in operation. Montana had 289, Colorado 1,518, Nebraska 3,000.

Moonlight, of course, didn't know the actual numbers, but his trips around the state gave him a feel that no set of figures could provide. The 1890 Census would reveal a pattern of land ownership, one of an almost feudal nature, that would eventually help defeat Moonlight. Other than Nevada, Wyoming had the largest average ranch size in the nation with 586 acres, more than double that of its southern neighbor, Colorado.

The 1890 Census also revealed how few in Wyoming actually owned cattle or sheep. Agricultural jobs dominated the employment numbers; they involved 25 percent of the state's populace. But nearly half of those people were either employees (cowboys or farmhands) or grain farmers. Only 4,147 or 13 percent of Wyoming's population considered themselves stockmen. Those people not only controlled politics, but finances as well. In 1889, with $2 million of produce and grains, farmers couldn't hold a candle financially to ranchers, who, while still struggling to get back on their feet, had $33 million in valuation. Moonlight accurately saw that Wyoming's land "was slipping away from actual settlers." Power in Wyoming, he confessed in 1887, lay "in the hands of a few."

Not only did Moonlight have a political fight on his hands, but the very geography of Wyoming did not accommodate granger ideology. It has the second highest mean elevation of any state (at 6,700 it's just 100 feet below Colorado's mean).

As humorist Bill Nye described Wyoming; "The climate is erratic, eccentric and peculiar. The altitude is between 7,000-8,000 feet above the high water mark, so that during the winter, it does not snow much, we being above the snowline, but in the summer the snow clouds rise above us and thus the surprised and indignant agriculturist is caught in the middle of a July day with a terrific fall of snow, so that he is virtually compelled to wear snowshoes all through the haying season. This is annoying and fatiguing. The snowshoes tread down the grass ahead of him, and make his progress laborious; besides, he tangles his feet up in the windrows, and falls on his nose nine times out of a possible ten."

Stockmen did their best to keep farmers off what little tillable land existed. Wyoming cattlemen did not appreciate even the occasional homesteader. "Most individual cattlemen did everything in their power to keep Wyoming's soil from being broken by the farmer's plow," commented an 1884 *Report to the House Committee on Public Lands on the Unlawful Occupancy of the Public Lands.*

Take the case of William Justin Harsha, a clergyman seeking

solace in cerebrally taxing sermons. In 1905, he staked 160 acres near Middle Park, Colorado, about seventy-five miles south of the Wyoming border. Harsha wrote that cowboys would ride up and stare at him and his son as they settled in. Their look, said the reverend, was "what on earth are you doing here on *our* public land" (his emphasis). As a deterrent, cattlemen shot Harsha's dogs, ran off his colts, and rustled his cattle.

Apparently, rules set by the federal government for acquiring land worked against homesteaders. Francis Warren wrote in the *Cheyenne Daily Sun* on October 18, 1886, that "but two patents have been issued during the past year for public lands in Wyoming although thousands of bona fide settlers have fully complied with the land laws, made final proof and final payment and are now awaiting the tardy issuance of the patents to which they are so justly entitled."

The same year, Warren also fumed about the small public land allotments in his 1886 governor's message. "In Wyoming, leaving out a very limited area of land along the streams, 160 acres would scarcely support five full grown domestic animals."

Furthermore, cattlemen were able to convert economic power into political capital. In the history of the post-settlement west, no single interest so controlled a state legislature as stockmen did in Wyoming. From 1868 until Moonlight's term, the Wyoming Stock Growers Association was denied nothing. Lastly, Moonlight was hindered by a victory the stockmen had won on the federal level. Secretary of the Interior Lucius Quintus Cincinnatus Lamar overruled Land Commissioner William A. J. Sparks's strict rules for gaining patents under the Desert Land Act. Under Lamar's relaxed regulations, one did not have to actually raise crops to acquire land, just bring water to it. Wyoming stockmen were not gardeners, but were eager to use the act to acquire more grazing land.

In 1887 Moonlight ambitiously stated that the theme "*Land for the Landless* [his emphasis] ought to be as good for Wyoming as any other locality. A quarter of a million of honest, hard-working citizens ought to find homes in Wyoming before 1890 shall expire. Not only will they turn over the soil and in the way of food for man and beast make Wyoming more than self-sustaining, which is not the case now, but they will develop mineral interests and give Wyoming a boom. Small ranches will give more people more production of the soil—more cattle and ten times more wealth than the large ranches possibly can do."

The former Indian fighter calculated that he had the necessary power to rearrange the deck. Cleveland had shown he meant business when he dismissed Moonlight's two predecessors, Francis E. Warren and George Baxter, because they violated new federal fencing laws. Little did Moonlight know that Warren had plans for him, to whit, taking satisfaction in "kicking [Moonlight] because he is an outsider."

Moonlight's Jeffersonian reckonings were in error. The 1888 and 1889 legislature antagonized its Democratic governor, thwarting him at almost every turn. They seemed especially delighted in stepping on his power of appointment. Moonlight, in turn, fought fire with fire, and vetoed bills that were not precisely to his liking. Warren and the stockmen made no bones about their feelings for Moonlight. "We ought to bounce this fellow," wrote Warren to fellow republican Robert Carey on March 17, 1888, "and take the chance of getting worse."

Any lingering trust Moonlight had in regional politics died during his Wyoming tenure. In a somewhat self-righteous booklet published in 1889, titled *Seven Vetoes*, he confessed that he feared "the selfish spirit of locality." He became a Western territory's bad dream: a governor who believed in a strong federal presence. To that end, he did not think Wyoming was ready for statehood and made his opinion known. He could not have given graver offense.

Wyoming did not accommodate Moonlight's bucolic vision of an agrarian paradise. Benjamin Harrison removed him from office in 1889 and appointed Francis Warren as territorial governor. Wyoming still lacked farmers and stockmen were in control.

To the last, Moonlight believed in the rectitude of his cause. His achievement was hiring Elwood Mead as Wyoming territorial water engineer. Mead managed to buck the stockmen's proclivity for giving private property rights from public domain commodities. Rather, Mead successfully campaigned to make all flowing water the property of the state. Water rights—the right to use water for irrigation when you need it—could not be bought and sold like a commodity. Instead, such rights were tied to the land. This put large and small landowners on relatively equal footing and had profound egalitarian consequences in a dry and arid state.

In reading his letters and speeches, it's clear that Moonlight could not abide embellishment. His frugal nature demanded understated and conservative calculations. This attribute, more than his gratingly antagonistic attitude toward ranching, offended Wyoming republicans. The territory was gearing for statehood and was intolerant of someone pointing out shortcomings, including lack of people.

Before he was removed, Moonlight informed the Interior Department that Wyoming's population was only 55,500, far short of the 130,000 required for statehood. Francis Warren estimated it at 85,000. The 1890 Census showed the actual population to be much closer to Moonlight's tally: 60,705.

Moonlight, therefore, must have winced at the picture Rep. Joseph M. Carey painted for his congressional colleagues. The image was Moonlight's dream, one that the republicans in the territory had done everything to thwart. Wyoming was, Carey said, "rich in agricultural possibilities." Twelve million acres could be irrigated. Mountain water, rich in nutrients, would perennially fertilize the field. "Tame grasses, timothy, alfalfa and clover, and wheat, oats, barley, rye, potatoes, melons, garden vegetables, berries and other small fruits and hardy varieties of apples are being successfully and generally grown." The population, continued Carey, was between 110,000 and 125,000.

What Moonlight could not have known was that Wyoming was about to embark on one of the most dismal economic development campaigns in U.S. history. Embellishments such as Carey's were to become the state's stock-in-trade. No state and governor could be more incompatible. As man and institution, their only common ground was poverty.

When he was removed, there was not enough left of his governor's $2,700 annual salary to move his family back to Kansas. Moonlight was forced to raise funds and was reduced to buying second-class fares. Yet, as he was purchasing tickets, a rival republican stopped him and inquired why the former executive of Wyoming would travel in such a fashion. Moonlight explained his predicament. The republican found this unacceptable and offered a loan. After some hedging, Moonlight accepted and offered his watch as collateral, which was refused. A little over two months later, Moonlight sent the republican a draft, repaying the loan with interest.

IV

MISSION IMPROBABLE

We don't know much about Roy W. Schenck. Wyoming archives and libraries have few records on him. Only his annual reports and sundry letters and telegrams survive, a singular oddity in that he was Wyoming's Commissioner of Immigration from 1911 to 1913.

His office received and wrote tens of thousands of letters; all but a few have vanished. Where and when he was born, what sort of family he had, what sort of suits he wore, and where he took his final breath, are conjecture. On the day he was sworn into office, Wyoming newspapers missed the event and focused on the starving elk herd in Jackson. Schenck was, for all practical purposes, an immigration czar who disappeared.

But from the scant documents he left, we can deduce that he was busy and distressed. He'd been hired on April 20, 1911, by the Wyoming State Board of Immigration. The eleventh state legislature created this department to promote immigration and "in general, further the advertising of the State." The previous immigration department had "failed to fulfill the purpose for which it was created in 1907," said Joseph Carey in a 1910 speech.

By now Wyoming was, at least on the surface, frantic for farmers. People were passing the state by. "Idaho, Washington and Oregon are filling up with people that go right through our State without knowing of its valuable resources," complained W. T. Judkins, Schenck's predecessor in the immigration department.

In crop agriculture, a critical gap lay between Wyoming and

neighboring states. At the height of what is considered to be the golden era of American agriculture (1890-1913) Wyoming produced little (only $10 million worth of grains and hay in 1910, for example). Nebraska produced $200 million the same year. If there ever was a time for Wyoming to make money in agriculture, this was it. Tariffs protected the tillers of the soil and the state had friends in high places.

But in 1910, Colorado produced five times more grains than Wyoming. Except for Nevada, Wyoming in 1910 had the smallest number of truck farms—those under fifty acres—in the nation with 645. By comparison, Utah had 5,550 and Colorado 3,882. Even for those homesteading a quarter-section (160 acres), Wyoming was behind. In 1910, Wyoming only had 3,800 residents with farms and ranches under 175 acres. Colorado had 16,300, Nebraska, 43,916.

Schenck took his charge seriously. Troubled by previous lackluster and halfhearted attempts to lure settlers to Wyoming, he was determined that his immigration efforts not fail. He created a database of facts and figures that might interest the potential immigrant or entrepreneur. No possible source escaped his attention. He collected information and data about Wyoming from colleges, land offices, cattlemen, railroads, newspapers, the federal government, and oil businesses, inaugurating "a system for the handling of statistics in a modern filing cabinet."

Integrity seemed the watchword. "We will give you reliable, unprejudiced information at any time upon any subject that you may wish," Schenck wrote. Indeed, the Board of Immigration passed a resolution stating that "fraudulent promotion schemes should be deplored and condemned by every public-spirited citizen of the State of Wyoming."

Yet for all his organization and propriety, Schenck could not squelch his speculator's tongue. He engaged in the very act he and the board professed to detest: that of exaggeration. Schenck described Wyoming in the superlative. "There is absolutely no question as to the fertility of the soil in Wyoming. It is rich and will produce enormous yields as compared with farms of the Middle West," he boasted in a pamphlet. Furthermore, he wrote, "put your crop proceeds into stock, dairy cattle, poultry, etc., and you will find that the way your bank account grows will exceed your most sanguine expectations."

A 1912 Wyoming Map of Resources claimed that Wyoming

alfalfa grown by irrigation "makes the hens cackle and the turkeys gobble. It induces pigs to squeal and grunt with satisfaction. It causes the dairy cow to give pailsful of creamy milk and makes the steer bawl for the feed rack. It softens the disposition of the colt, fattens the lambs, fertilizes the soil, and fills the pockets of the farms with gold."

Using the $500 per month the Board gave him to advertise, Schenck placed ads in Eastern newspapers and magazines. One extolling Wyoming horticultural prowess read:

"Wyoming Fruit Land—Will grow Apples, Pears, Cherries, Plums, Small Fruits, Cantaloupes, Water Melons and Vegetables which bring highest prices. Irrigated Land $25 to $100 per acre. Tracts to suit. Small Payment, easy terms. Crops will quickly pay for land. Plenty of water for irrigation. Rich virgin soil."

This was, remember, the same land that in 1888 Bill Nye facetiously, but not inaccurately, spoke about as having snowfall twelve months out of the year. But Schenck's campaign spurred the hopeful. "More than 42,000 letters have been written during the past 18 months in replying to inquiries and in sending information to those whose addresses have been furnished by others," he said in an annual report. "According to the card index filing system in this office, all inquiries are recorded on a card which shows the name of the correspondent, his file number, dates of his letters, and all correspondence and literature that has been sent to him."

His office wrote and disseminated sixty-four pieces of literature on dry farming, obtaining free government land, tourism, raising hogs, starting a dairy, raising fruits. It printed 125,000 copies of a four-color "resource map" pointing out Wyoming's bounty. Its theme: *The New Wyoming: The Land of Great Rewards.*

Schenck didn't limit promotions to mail and advertising alone. He spent $7,000 and hired a special train car to bring out fifteen correspondents—"brilliant writers"—from Eastern newspapers. The Immigration Board wined and dined them at Cheyenne's Industrial Club, "royally entertained" them at the Chapman Brothers's ranch outside Evanston, packed the writers for ten days in Yellowstone National Park, then through Cody, over the Bighorns into Sheridan and finally south back to Cheyenne.

Road trips to conventions and land shows took up Schenck's time. At Chicago, New York, and Pittsburgh land shows, the Board of Immigration set up an exhibit titled "Wyoming, The Land of Great Reward," complete with a wall of produce and two stuffed elk heads. Schenck estimated that in the three cities, more than a million people visited the Wyoming exhibit. The Board gave away 200,000 pieces of literature about the Land of Great Reward. As a promotion it gave away two tracts of irrigated land with a fully paid up water right.

According to the memoirs of future Wyoming governor Leslie A. Miller, who worked with Schenck for a spell, his boss was of dynamic personage, "able as a showman," but "had little or no sense of responsibility," and, if we are to believe Miller's inference, a lady's man.

"I have never seen people more interested in anything than those who hear my lectures every day, seem to be in Wyoming," wrote Schenck to Carey on October 28, 1911, about the Pittsburgh show.

Carey responded to this enthusiasm by calls for economy. Schenck promised to minimize expenses. "I shall cut down my office force to our stenographer upon completion of the Land Shows," he pledged the governor on November 11, 1911.

While most of the letters from potential immigrants addressed to Schenck and his office are lost, some addressed to Governor Carey survive. They wanted just what Wyoming promoted. In a handwritten note using pencil on 8x5 lined paper, Carl Olson of Vilas, Kansas, inquired on December 4th, 1913: "Have you any homestead land, subject to entry, close to railroad and city, where rainfall is sufficient to raise crops without irrigation?"

Another Kansas resident wrote: "I want to start a little ranch or dairy; would like to get in on some good valley near a stream if possible and some timber. Does the wind flow up in those counties? That's the trouble here. Too much wind."

Others wished to flee their own agricultural troubles. "I am a young man and have a nice home near the city of Meridian in the cotton growing region. But the Boll-weevil is ruining the cotton in our State. I would like to exchange my farm for property in the west," said R. V. House, Meridian, Mississippi.

Schenck also began pushing what a bargain could be had in the state, and, in fact, may have started Wyoming's tradition of bottom-

Wyoming alfalfa: An example of early (1912) Wyoming agricultural boosterism. This alfalfa "makes the hens cackle and the turkeys gobble. It induces pigs to squeal and grunt with satisfaction. It causes the dairy cow to give pailsful of creamy milk and makes the steer bawl for the feed rack. It softens the disposition of the colt, fattens the lambs, fertilizes the soil, and fills the pockets of the farms with gold."

feeding. "I believe that if you come to Wyoming you will find far greater opportunities than you can obtain in the east.," Schenck wrote to Harold Fish of Paterson, New Jersey on January 1, 1912. Properties were a deal. "...lands in Wyoming are twice to twenty times as cheap as they are in other states of the Rocky Mountain region."

Homesteads may have been a bargain, but they were not Wyoming's to give away. Schenck's office promoted settlement of land the state did not control. With the exception of the Carey Act, which indeed gave the State Land Office a say in settlement of arid lands, homesteaders had to go through the six federal land offices located throughout Wyoming. Repeatedly, Carey wrote potential immigrants, "you are advised that the Government lands open for entry within this State are under the jurisdiction of the United States Land Office."

In what was already a Wyoming tradition of blaming the federal government for its problems, Schenck complained. "Rulings and reversal of rulings by the Land Department have made it extremely difficult, and in many instances practically impossible for a homesteader or investor to secure title to certain lands within our borders or to start developing any wealth they may contain.

Irrigation, mining, lumbering and power development in this State will be practically at a standstill until a new policy is adopted," said Schenck in his 1912 annual report.

The Wyoming legislature's patience with the Board of Immigration waned. Schenck, in fact, was forced into mendicancy and in March 21, 1912, pleaded with Gerrit Fort of Wyoming's long-time benefactor, the Union Pacific, to donate $5,000 to the Immigration Board. Schenck even tried to coax "Hebrew Colonists" with eighty-acre parcels outside Wheatland.

By the time Schenck got to his biennial report in 1913, hesitation and bitterness crept into his writing. People were reading his literature, but rarely acting on it. He could not assuage rejection's sting. Using what he termed "conservative figures," Schenck calculated that Wyoming had unused resources totaling $47 billion and yet assessed valuation of only $185 million. "Wyoming," he wrote, "has anything but an enviable reputation among prospective homeseekers, immigrants and investors. This undesirable impression apparently has been growing greater instead of less."

"What is the matter?" he wondered aloud then gave his hypothesis, which was lack of proper information. The people of Wyoming "have allowed outsiders to gain their only knowledge of the state through reading lurid tales of the barrenness of our deserts, the outlawry of our citizens and the general undesirability of the state."

Schenck evinced a gnawing insecurity that has infected Wyoming state officials ever since. With all these potential riches, why won't people live here? What Schenck wanted was what Wyoming couldn't seem to support: small, independent farmers and ranchers.

In desperation, Schenck concocted one last plan: act as a land bank. The state should buy federal land then sell irrigated, 80-acre farms to settlers, on "liberal terms of payment."

"A home would be ready for the settler and his family immediately upon their arrival in Wyoming."

Promotion provided the main advantage of this plan. "Wyoming would be the first state in the Union to adopt such a plan [and it] would provide the widest publicity to the project." He furthermore said that Wyoming should employ a man "conversant in several languages" to meet immigrants who have landed at the port of New York.

The Wyoming legislature, however, was in no mood for such aspirations or largess. Not only did it fail to fund Schenck's request but it denied any money whatsoever for the Office of Immigration. Schenck, his job now gone, disappeared. The correspondence of 42,000 inquiries, vanished. Carey blamed his colleagues in the house and senate. He replied to an inquiry about the board, "since our last legislature made no appropriation for the Immigration Board, the Commissioner is not now at work."

The Board of Immigration enjoyed a brief resurrection in 1919, notable only in that Commissioner Charles Hill complained that "Wyoming has suffered from the unscrupulous methods employed by agents of the Canadian government and railroads, and land men from other sections, who have sold land such as the Florida Everglades, etc."

Like his predecessors and those to come after him, Hill pushed the potential of facts. "As every good business man must make an inventory, so should the state." And more boosterism. "With a great area of splendid tillable land; with an abounding and diversified wealth of mineral resources, unequaled in any other section of the United States; with beauty as rare and scenery as grand as can be found in the known world, Wyoming is indeed a land of diversity and progress, possessing at the close of 1922, greater possibilities for future development than any other western state," wrote Hill in his annual report. "The fertile soil and inexhaustible quantity of water for irrigation insure the success of agriculture for all time to come."

By then, however, Wyoming, which had enjoyed brief prosperity during the war, was about to plunge into a depression that lasted twenty years. But the die was cast and theories hardened from opinion into fact: as a state, Wyoming could do little to attract successful small farmers or businesses. Rather, it had to depend upon immigration incentives from the federal government.

At a time when what farmers had to offer sold for next to nothing, new tillers of the soil did indeed come to Wyoming. The Dry Homestead Act of 1909 and the Grazing Homestead Act of 1916 were crucibles of heartbreak. For most of these new immigrants, as Everett Dick pointed out, "the point of starvation would be reached before the culmination of the five-year required residence."

V

AN AWFUL SENSE OF PATIENCE

On an August afternoon in 1924, Parke Fox and his brother Dale walked through the sagebrush towards their parents's homestead south of Rosette, Wyoming. The late afternoon sun dried their backs, damp with the sweat of exertion. The brothers, ages fifteen and eighteen, had just spent eight days hand-stacking millet for a neighboring rancher. They earned $0.25 for each eight-hour day. That afternoon they had completed the task and been paid: two silver dollars apiece.

After they'd walked about a mile, Dale stopped and turned to Parke. "Let me carry your two dollars for a little while. I just want to know how it feels to carry four dollars."

Parke hesitated. He'd never possessed such wealth. The clank of those two dollars in his pocket, he would recall seventy-seven years later, was the grandest sound he'd ever heard in his life.

"C'mon," his brother said. "In a little bit, I'll give 'em back to you plus my two dollars so you know what it feels like to carry all that money."

Parke obliged. The two continued walking home, swapping the money each mile and reveling in their new affluence. They had to cross the Belle Fourche river on a down log. "You can bet we clamped on to those coins when we crawled across that log," said Parke.

The Fox family had left Wilmore, Kansas, on March 27th, 1917, to move to a 360-acre homestead. Parke's father, a struggling black-smith, decided to try his hand at farming. He rented a railroad car and loaded it with their possessions: a milk cow, horse and colt, a

.22 rifle, a walking plow, disc, and mattresses. Parke and Dale hid in the manger of the boxcar, successfully evading the fare from Wilmore to Moorcroft, Wyoming. Their mother and younger brothers and sisters rode in the passenger cars.

On March 30th they arrived in Moorcroft with $35 to their name. A former neighbor from Kansas, Jake Dillinger, who had homesteaded two years earlier, met them with a team at the station. It was bitterly cold, approaching twenty below zero. Dillinger drove them eighteen miles to his dugout. When crossing a creek the wagon broke through the ice. Dillinger walked into the water and pushed them out, his boots and pantlegs freezing instantly. That night, both families, totaling four adults and eight children, all slept on the packed earth floor of the Dillingers's ten by fourteen cabin.

The next morning, Dillinger drove the Fox family to their new home. The Foxes had never seen their acquisition. It had been swapped sight unseen for their home in Kansas. As Parke would describe it, it was little more than a hole in the ground, three feet deep, with a shed over the top of it. There was no door, just a square hole at the bottom of crumbling earthen steps. One entered the building backwards, on hands and knees, and stepped onto an apple box. Its dirt floor never acquired a covering during the Foxes' homestead tenure.

Destitution haunted the family. Parke said, "my mother would tip up the mattresses on their side during the day so we'd have some space to move around. There was a stove and a little table. My brother and I'd go hunting and kill a hare once in a while. That'd be the only source of meat we'd have. Sometimes we'd shoot a sage grouse, which was illegal at the time. In the summertime, we'd go gather lamb's quarter [a tall weed whose pale green leaves can be cooked like spinach] and sometimes that's all we'd eat for a week."

That fall, it snowed four inches on September 2nd. "We didn't see the ground again until April," said Parke.

By 1917, most of the good open homesteading land had been taken. Federal legislation supposedly created to help the very homesteader Roy Schenck wanted instead produced opportunities for cattlemen already on the land. The Grazing Homestead Act of 1916 did, in fact, little for immigrants seeking land. The Cheyenne Land Office noted that of the 1,250 homestead filings during the first two weeks of January 1917, most were completed by Wyoming residents "for the purpose of squaring up ranches."

Latecomers got little of what they needed most: water. Parke and his brother had the chore of fetching this necessity from the Belle Fourche River, two miles away. "At that time, it was a running river. Now there ain't hardly anything left," he said. They hooked up the team—a mare and her barely containable colt—loaded three empty wooden barrels on the wagon, then returned with them filled.

They earned a living any way they could. "When our milk cow would freshen, we'd go sell the [local] rancher milk at ten cents a gallon," said Parke. His father worked as an itinerant blacksmith, repairing plows and other farm equipment. Desperate for funds, Parke, Dale, and their father undertook the grim job of gathering wool off dead sheep. For three months, they scoured the hillsides for winter-killed sheep. They salvaged $115 worth of wool, then split the proceeds fifty/fifty with the owner of the sheep.

Tough and resourceful, they used what others left behind. When a neighboring homesteader gave up trying to make the land pay, he gave the Fox family permission to take his house. In fact, they benefited this way twice. Each time, the Foxes loaded a little home up on their wagon, carried it back to their homestead and attached it to the existing building.

They made do without basic necessities. When Parke's horse slipped on a clay riverbank, the fall pinned Parke and broke his leg just above the ankle. His father inspected the break, then asked Dale to fetch some bits of wood and steel baling wire. He reset Parke's bones, then bound the break with a splint of wood and wire. A year later, Parke's father broke his leg; Parke and Dale set it in the same manner. The appendages of both father and son healed without incident. Parke once drove the team to Moorcroft in March to pick up hay. He had outgrown his boots, so to protect his feet against cold, he wrapped them in gunny sacks bound with wire.

Parke began breaking horses at age sixteen. "I was supposed to do it for five dollars a head, but it seems I rarely ever got more than two dollars."

Parke recalled his moment of wonder when he dispatched—with a pistol—a running antelope while sitting in the saddle of a galloping horse. "What are the chances of that?" he still marvels. "It was a green horse, too, and he didn't much like me blasting away up there with my .30 caliber Luger." The horse didn't care for the dead antelope, which Parke gutted, then tried to tie behind the saddle. "Eventually, I figured out how to do it: I took off my shirt and blindfolded the horse. Then, slowly, I got that antelope tied up behind the saddle. Then I got on the horse and eased the blindfold off him. He jumped around a bit, but I hung on."

Parke may have been able to stay in the saddle, but holding on to the homestead was another matter. The poverty wore too thin. Parke's two sisters moved to Sheridan and began waitressing. They rented a house for $15.00 a month. After settling in, they moved their parents off the homestead into town. Parke and his brothers followed. It was 1926. Their dream—the dream Wyoming so badly wanted to work—a viable homestead—abandoned.

I tried to find the Fox homestead. A three-hour search in July heat revealed no evidence of a home. The land wasn't hospitable towards agriculture. Sagebrush and prickly pear cactus, some in bloom, covered most of the land. Cheat grass, with its spermatozoa-shaped seeds, burrowed into my socks. Only the coulees were thick with grass. I searched for signs of human habitation—boards, metal objects, old stove or stove pipe or any indentations in the earth. Did the Foxes snuggle in against the shade of a cottonwood tree, by chance?

I thought they might want a place set against the hillside that was near the creek, but not so close they'd get flooded out in a gully washer. They would seek the protection of the hillside against the northwest wind and snow, but not too snug against the hills lest the May runoff end up on the floor.

Spring rains erode land, especially when disturbed by livestock. Weather took or hid whatever remains of the Fox home. The inventory at the end of my search consisted of a decrepit galvanized bucket and a relatively new oil drum. Badger holes, cottontails, and a three-point mule deer in velvet concluded my list of observations.

The Fox family saga repeated itself throughout the state. In fact, more families filed for homesteads in the 1920s than any other time in Wyoming history. They abandoned them. Without timber or water, they faced the same fate as the Foxes. From 1919 to 1929, approximately 50,000 people filed for seventeen million acres of homestead land in Wyoming. On the surface, this would confirm

Wyoming Wants Farmers	**Wyoming at a Glance** The Land of Great Reward	Wyoming Wants Capital

Area, 62,460,160 acres.

 10,000,000 acres of irrigated land open, or projected.

 35,000,000 acres open to homesteaders.

Population. Wyoming has room for 1,000,000 people. Census of 1910 showed 145,965.

Coal. 425 billion tons of workable high grade coal, according to U. S. Geological Survey, or 1-7 of the entire estimated tonnage of the United States.

 $11,706,187 worth of coal mined in 1910.

 Coal mines in every county save one.

Oil. 7 of 14 counties have producing wells. 4 other counties have oil but no transportation facilities.

Iron. 150 carloads of ore shipped each day from one district. Iron deposits almost inexhaustible.

Farming. Farm lands gained in value 279% between 1900 and 1910. Irrigated land costs $25 to $75 per acre.

 Fruit. 150,000 apple trees planted during last season in Big Horn Basin alone. Fruit land costs $25 to $75 an acre.

 Hog Raising. Alfalfa is the best hog feed known. Excellent local market. Hog cholera absolutely unknown.

 Dairying. Alfalfa is the best dairy food. 15 creameries in state. Excellent local market for dairy products. Cheap land makes dairying profitable.

 Sugar Beets. Beet growers in Wyoming this year netted $41 to $73 an acre on land costing $25 to $75 an acre. Beet sugar factories wanted.

 General Farming. Grains, vegetables, etc., give wonderful yields.

Minerals. Gold, silver, copper, lead, tin, zinc, asbestos, graphite, natural gas, cement, plaster, granite, marble, sandstone, limestone, brick clay, shale, onyx, gypsum, sulphur, phosphate rock, etc.

Water Power. Unlimited. Wyoming has more water than any other western state. Power sites sufficient for more factories than in all the New England States.

Tourists. Scenery unexcelled, both in Yellowstone Park and in every mountain range in the state. Roads excellent for automobiles.

Hunting and Fishing. 25,000 wild elk, deer, bear, mountain sheep, sage chickens, etc. Best trout fishing in U. S. 300 days of sunshine per year. Climate unsurpassed. Air invigorating and health giving.

Educational facilities. Good schools everywhere. State University at Laramie.

For information write,

WYOMING PUBLICITY ASSOCIATION CHEYENNE, WYOMING

STATE BOARD OF IMMIGRATION CHEYENNE, WYOMING

Land of Great Rewards: Flyer published by Wyoming State Board of Immigration, probably around 1912. Despite an impressive list of assets, capitalists and farmers generally went elsewhere.

or validate the work of Schenck and the State Board of Immigration. It's precisely such numbers that fuel Wyoming's pioneer myth. For once, farmers outranked ranchers. A 1925 census compiled by the state showed 8,222 ranchers and 11,267 farmers.

By the end of the 1920s, the dream vanished. From 1919 to 1929, the number of existing ranches and farms in Wyoming rose less than 1 percent, from 15,748 to 16,011, or 263 total. Simultaneously, the average acreage for ranches doubled. Most homestead land did not end up in the hands of small agricultural operations; it was either abandoned or used to enlarge extant ranches. The 1930

Census showed that 95 percent of Wyoming remained unplowed and 80 percent of the cash receipts came from stock raising.

The 1920s were awful years for Wyoming agriculture. Deflation and dropping prices for all commodities caused even large operations to suffer. Wheat prices sank from $2.43 per bushel in 1919 to $0.92 in 1922. Cattle values dropped 71 percent from 1919 to 1926, a year in which the number of beef cattle sunk to a record low of 281,000. Agriculture made up the largest section of the state's assessed valuation, employed half the population, and yet it could not pay the bills. This clearly worried the state's new democratic governor.

In 1933, Leslie Miller sat in his office pondering the state's condition. Miller was about to make history. A self-educated former Marine Corps drill sergeant who made his own bed and breakfast each morning, Miller concluded he would not support the image Wyoming insisted on pinning on its chest: a state too enthralled with its independent image to ask for help. Miller would tell the legislature that Wyoming needed and would request federal assistance.

It was not a position conjured overnight. Miller, a lover of gardenias and dahlias, had the reputation as a tough, independent man who took neither guff nor largess, least of all from the federal government. He loathed pork. Later in life when appointed to the Hoover Commission's Natural Resource Board (which investigated federally funded water and energy projects), Miller spoke critically of the Columbia Valley Authority, the Army Corps of Engineers, and various flood control projects.

In short, Miller was a man who spoke his mind. But his eleven months in office had provided a sobering education on self-sufficiency. He'd already spoken candidly to the legislature twice that year. In his first speech, he revealed that the general fund was overdrawn by $563,000; state investments in agriculture were not doing well. Wyoming had invested $2.4 million of common school funds in drainage and irrigation bonds. "We now have a total of $140,644.09 in unpaid interest on these bonds and $30,900 on the principal payments," said Miller. Investments from the Farm Loan Board were in trouble. Loans delinquent sixty days constituted 40 percent of the total funds invested. He questioned the need for future loans. In 1928, his republican predecessor Governor Frank Emerson, blithely reported that "good business methods are now employed in handling the Farm Loan Board business of the state."

Emerson, in fact, had gone as far as recommending an additional $1 million in the Farm Loan Board's Revolving Fund. This was at a time when, by Emerson's own admission, Utah, Montana, Idaho, and South Dakota were suffering from bad farm loans. In 1928, South Dakota's farm loan system reported a $5 million loss.

During his second speech to the legislature on January 17th, Miller detailed more problems. "The delinquent tax list of 1932 was on the whole the largest in the history of the state and figures which are coming from a number of counties indicate the situation will be incomparably worse," he said. Counties owned $14 million in property purchased at tax sales. The Poor and Pauper Fund of almost every county was overdrawn. Miller hinted, but did not say until later, that he wanted cooperation with the federal government, especially with the National Recovery Act.

It's easy to understand Miller's hesitation, both on a personal and state level. Asking Wyoming to participate in the National Recovery Act was, as Wyoming historian T. A. Larson would describe in his essay *The New Deal in Wyoming,* "revolutionary." While Miller had worked for the federal government—at one time he was the first IRS Commissioner in Wyoming—his frugal and independent nature cringed at the thought of a handout. Historian James Patterson called Miller "thrifty, unventuresome, and very conscious of the anti-New Deal attitudes of his new constituents."

Miller would eventually conclude that New Deal expenditures had gotten entirely out of hand. But in Wyoming, a request to cooperate with Washington was a solicitation to collaborate with the devil. In fact, Wyoming historian Roy Jordan avers the state's antigovernment sentiment is of a theological nature. "In Wyoming, it's a religion. It's a real religion," said Jordan.

By the time Miller got to his third speech of the year, he was ready to become an apostate. For the sake of maintaining Wyoming's rugged reputation, a string of governors had misread Wyoming's economy and ignored what the Depression was doing to their constituency. Emerson said in January 1931 that "Wyoming is in comparatively good condition." Regrettably, the same diagnosis could not be made for Emerson himself, who died of a streptococcus infection a month after making that statement. His temporary fill-in, Alonzo Clark, declared in 1932 that Wyoming could take care of its unemployed.

It's important to point out how deeply in denial Wyoming was about its financial condition. Only loans kept the state from destitution. For eighteen years (1914-1932) this supposedly independent-minded state had been pouring borrowed money into agriculture while simultaneously permitting an exceedingly relaxed taxation policy concerning mineral and oil extraction. As Miller himself said in his memoirs, "The general fund of the state had been overdrawn [sic] in varying amounts, sometimes as much as $1,000,000, nearly all of the time since 1914. From 1925 to 1932, only nine scattered months [were found] that an overdraft had not existed. During the year I was elected, 1932, the daily average was $700,000. Approximately $350,000 in interest at 6 per cent was paid on this overdraft."

Like his democratic predecessor, Thomas Moonlight, Miller had a visceral sense of Wyoming conditions, one that numbers available to him at the time wouldn't necessarily verify. Miller had at one time worked for S.G. Hopkins, commissioner of public lands and as chief clerk in the state lands office. He traveled the state in this capacity, getting to know hundreds of ranchers, farmers and land productivity. As he wrote in his memoirs: "The dry farming venture proved fitful to many. Mortality was great. During the abnormally dry years of the 1930s, hundred and hundreds of dry farms were abandoned or sold to the federal government."

A low unemployment rate, officially 6.1 percent, did not dissuade Miller that Wyoming was in need of help. Figures compiled later by historians give credence to Miller's concerns about real poverty. For example, Wyoming ranchers endured a 60 percent drop in income from 1929 to 1932, one of the biggest losses among agricultural producers in the nation. Cattle values, on a per head basis, dropped from $59 in 1929 to $16 by 1934. In 1930, the Wyoming Stock Growers Association had a grand total of $565 in its bank account. The state, as a whole, suffered a 42 percent drop in per capita income from 1929 to 1932. While not unique (Montana had a 50 percent drop during the same period; North Dakota 59 percent), the Depression dealt Wyoming a hard hand. It nearly crushed not only agriculture, but the nascent oil industry as well.

Low demand caused much of oil's downfall. Yet the monopolistic nature of Wyoming's oil structure invited collapse. A special report written by the Federal Trade Commission in 1921 called Wyoming "the most important crude oil state in the Rocky Mountain region." The report also stated, "there is greater concentration in the control of crude petroleum in the Wyoming oil fields than in any other field in the United States."

The report estimated that Standard Oil of Indiana controlled upwards of 97 percent of Wyoming's crude oil production. This created great disparities of wealth. While Parke Fox and his family were living in a dirt-floored homesteader's cabin, the Midwest Refining Company, which was controlled by Standard Oil, enjoyed returns of 25 to 33 percent per annum.

While the economy did stabilize under Miller's hand, it did not improve much until 1939. Wyoming banks were going under like orchids in a snowstorm. Out of 153 banks doing business in 1920, only sixty-nine were left by 1933. Most of the banking damage occurred before Miller's time. With 20,000 unemployed, the state's revenue stream had been reduced to a trickle. One out of every five persons in Wyoming was receiving relief.

Those lucky enough to be employed were offered a pauper's wage. Robert Strahorn's *Handbook of Wyoming* reported that in 1877, cowboys were paid $32.50 per month, room and board. A half-century later, their wage hadn't changed. In 1933, cowboys and farm laborers were paid $1 a day, room and board. Coal miners, working at reduced wages, were earning $5.42 per day.

The conditions made staying in Wyoming a questionable undertaking. The temptation, especially for creative minds, was to leave. "Right now I'm impressed and saddened by the fact that no able lawyer has any business settling in Wyoming under present economic conditions," wrote Thurman Arnold in 1937 to his friend Joseph R. Sullivan of Laramie.

An individualistic, Laramie-born professor at Yale, Arnold had put aside academia to work as an antitrust investigator for the New Deal's Temporary National Economic Commission. Arnold continued, "If he has any sense at all, he will move to the Atlantic seaboard. That is not only true of lawyers but of university professors or anyone else who wants either money, intellectual contacts or anything else. Economic disadvantage creates a backward country."

But Wyoming could not acknowledge its poverty. The republican-controlled Senate killed a resolution calling for a special session of Congress to provide unemployment relief. Wyoming agriculture, however, was already accepting money from the federal government. It was not doing very well with it, either. In 1932, the federal government was able to collect only 1.2 percent of the $650,000 in loans it had given to Wyoming farmers and ranchers. Out of 3,437 loans, only thirty-four had been paid back in full.

The lack of farmers permitted Wyoming to entertain illusions of self-reliance. That was not the case in surrounding states, where farmers had turned into a potent and often quite radical political force. South in Colorado, 1,500 farmers marched on the Capitol in 1932 to protest land assessments. In 1934, 700-800 protestors stormed the state senate chambers in Denver, putting the solons in flight. In Idaho, C. Ben Ross won the governorship as a democrat in a conservative republican state. It was southwestern Idaho, the area an historian called the state's "traditional hotbed of agrarian radicalism," that carried Ross. In 1931, he passed an income tax. In 1932, the democrats took both of Idaho's congressional seats.

Under republicans and until Miller's time, Wyoming was the single state in the Union that did not borrow emergency relief money from the New Deal's Reconstruction Finance Corporation. The amount borrowed was to be repaid out of future federal highway funds. The state took pride in this but during this third and final speech in 1933, Miller confessed to the legislature, "I've been wondering recently whether we were entitled to indulge in that feeling of pride." Reliable sources, he continued, "have documented thousands of cases of undernourishment of children, and, likewise, many cases indicating a lack of proper clothing for both children and adults."

It was a plain and direct speech, one that demanded Wyoming to face its problems. "Accept the responsibility that is yours," Miller said.

They did. As T. A. Larson pointed out, the legislature "adopted a state recovery act and approved federal bank deposit insurance, federally financed homeowner's loans, federally aided state relief, public employment offices, public works financing, and a $300,000 federal loan for construction at the state university."

By 1935, the general fund had a $450,000 surplus, largely due to heavy federal intervention (Washington was spending between $30,000 and $35,000 per month in Wyoming) raising revenue, and

Miller's insistence on a spartan budget. For example, the governor himself cut his own salary in half while enacting a 2 percent sales tax, which provided $500,000 for public welfare.

Then Wyoming reverted to old habits. Miller was voted out, as was the democratic majority in the House and Senate. In came Nels Smith, a conservative Sundance rancher, as governor. With him and the new republican legislature came a flood of antigovernment and antitax vitriol. National price controls and rationing during WWII only exacerbated the situation.

Yet along with the red tape of war came fleeting prosperity. Wyoming's ranchers and farmers were finally, after twenty years of dust and destitution, able to make a decent living, if only for awhile.

Since statehood in 1890, Wyoming wanted to show itself it could survive without federal government money. But it had to admit, in what could be described as self-disgust, that its economy, so dependent on natural resources, was inextricably linked to policy made in Washington. The state could no longer hide its reliance on federal money, especially after 1934. That year Wyoming stockmen took 63 percent, or $6.8 million, of the loans from the Federal Land Bank in Omaha. And yet they fumed when the Taylor Grazing Act of 1934 created five grazing districts in the state. The Wyoming Stock Growers Association called it another "bureaucratic powergrab."

Meanwhile, the federal Public Works Administration paid for structures that were to become symbols of Wyoming: the State Supreme Court Building in Cheyenne (45 percent of the funding came from the federal government; the remainder came from selling state lands held in trust for education purposes) and the Student Center at the University of Wyoming. From 1935 to 1939 the Rural Electric Association ran power to 2773 farms and ranches. In 1931, there were only 351 miles of paved or oiled roads in Wyoming. That changed to 3,400 miles by 1939, giving Wyoming one of the highest percentages of hard-surfaced roads in the nation. Wyoming led the country in per capita Farm Security Administration loans at $30 per person. When the Depression-era programs ended in 1940, Wyoming had taken $142 million from Washington, more per capita than any other state save Montana and Nevada.

The fable of the independent rancher or homesteader could no longer stand. Wyoming quickly buried the Depression. Other states, such as Oklahoma, Kansas, the Dakotas, acknowledge the Depression and incorporate the era into their history. In Wyoming, the Depression remains unexamined. No writer outside of academic circles has explored the Great Depression and its effects on the state. Not a single article in *The Annals of Wyoming*, the official organ of Wyoming history, discusses the socioeconomic ramifications. The one exception is T. A. Larson who, in various publications, including the *History of Wyoming*, discusses the topic. Larson, however, tends to concentrate on the New Deal rather than the Depression itself.

Those who do examine Wyoming's Depression are often surprised at its length and severity, as well as the role of the federal government. One master's candidate at the University of Wyoming put it this way. "In reappraising the facts and statistics on Wyoming construction from 1935-1940, one can't help but be appalled by the dominant part the federal government played in stimulating construction in Wyoming—construction which gave employment and lasting benefits to the state during the period of crisis."

Roy Jordan, a retired history professor from Northwest College, explains the absence of commentary this way: as bad as the Depression was, the hardship wasn't new to Wyoming. "Wyoming's always been under a depression. So why should we write about it?"

Federal expenditures in the state were not out of line. The New Deal distributed $2.5 billion in New York, $1.8 billion in Pennsylvania, and $1.1 billion in Texas. Wyoming's $142 million appears downright reasonable and is a fraction of Nevada's ($1,130), Montana, ($710) per capita spending.

No other state—perhaps with the exception of Nevada—had so much riding on its image. Wyoming was, and remains, utterly attached to its idea of independence. The Depression shattered that illusion. Sixty years of boosterism and fabrication finally caught up with the state. In 1930, Wyoming had 326 post offices—near its historical peak. Twenty years later, 125 of these were gone. The Depression swallowed towns like Badwater, Dad, Ishawooa, Tipperary, Burnt Fork, Kleenburn, Difficulty, Soda Well, Fossil, Verse, and Little Medicine. As Wyoming peered into the future, it didn't much like what it saw: forced cooperation with the federal government, a tough vision for a state that saw its salvation in natural resources—most of which it did not own.

VI

INVENTION

He was a flashy sorrel named Redwing. An Indian, a Crow or Cheyenne, sold the horse as a colt to George Ostrom at the Sheridan Rodeo for $10.00 in 1913. During WWI, Ostrom took Redwing with him to his army camp in Cheyenne. Too young for a remount, Redwing survived the army because Ostrom got himself assigned to loading stock cars. When the brass turned their head, Ostrom loaded Redwing in with the other regular army remounts.

But at Charlotte, North Carolina, the army separated Redwing and Ostrom. They both went to France but owner and horse did not meet again until after the war. Ostrom fought with the 148th Field Artillery. While there, the command at Chateau-Thierry held a contest for a design to represent the regiment. Inspired by his long-lost mount, Ostrom took aside a marching drum. On the drumhead, he painted Redwing in the midst of a full buck. The task was interrupted by shell fire, as Ostrom told the story. The design won the day and from then on the 148th was known as the bucking bronc outfit from Wyoming.

Redwing, it turned out, did not face fire on the front lines. Rather, he enjoyed fine surroundings. His demeanor and looks brought the attention of the French School of Equitation in Tours. After the war, Ostrom wanted to bring him back to Wyoming, but could not afford the $1,500 shipping charge. He sold Redwing to the school, where the horse presumably remained until death.

But in the minds of Wyomingites, he lives forever, for Redwing is the inspiration for Wyoming's bucking bronco. The emblem was later redesigned by Denver resident Allen True, who used A. J. "Stub" Farlow of Lander struggling to hold on to a bronc named Steamboat.

In 1935, Secretary of State Lester Hunt put the bucking bronco on the state license plate, conveniently attaching the copyright in his name.

He did so "because it would not highlight any particular locality or event since rodeos were common all over the state." The *Wyoming State Journal* reported that Hunt liked the idea because "the new plate is not only symbolic of our State, but it also carries with it a definite advertising value for Wyoming.... He [the rider on the bucking bronco] represents all that is typical and symbolic of the West."

In territorial times, as T.A. Larson said, baseball was more important than rodeos, "which were rare and unimportant." Thus Hunt chose, for reasons of promotion, a relative newcomer. This may have been because Hunt was from Lander, the town that sponsored Wyoming's first paid rodeo with its "Pioneer Days" in 1894. And by the 1930s many Wyoming towns did, in fact, have their own rodeo. Hunt's reluctance to promote any one locality was admirable, for he knew Wyoming residents to be touchy about regionalism. It distorted, however, and institutionalized a thin section of history.

Wyoming's fight for survival cast a long and indelible shadow over the state. The state's collective memory still recalled Grant's attempt to pull the plug. What saved the state in the late 1870s would again come to the rescue: cattle. It didn't matter that the livestock industry was on its knees. The image, at least, could be resurrected. Wyoming began to reinvent itself. It forgot the collapse of cattle in 1887, the poverty brought on by agriculture, and its struggles to attract truly independent figures: farmers, entrepreneurs, and successful homesteaders. Instead, it created a romantic past of the wild West, a remarkable figure: the rugged, independent, individualistic cowboy.

As University of Wyoming historian Phil Roberts explains, "the [accepted story] of individualism—the historical myth—which doesn't have a great deal of foundation, is that Wyoming was settled by individuals who acted independently and without government help and without intervention. You take a look at the historical record and that's not the case. Wyoming started as the result of huge corporations and everyone who was involved in that early period were all dependent on that corporation. Your individuals—the ones who actually settled here—homesteaded on federal lands. Through federal help they gained their piece of the pie. Lots of those people took advantage of loopholes in the land laws and were able to build small empires. Then to say that individuals came out here with a horse and running iron and a rope and built the state from scratch is not an accurate portrayal."

Wyoming's romantic reinvention actually began in the 1890s, when the young state was trying to find its sense of purpose. Cheyenne's Frontier Days, organized in 1897 to compete with Greeley, Colorado's "Potato Days," attracted national attention by the 1920s. It was "The Greatest Frontier Celebration on Earth," and in 1925 was described as "a Wyoming institution, a powerful influence in making men mindful of the spirit and traditions of this country."

This is heady language—already dripping with mythological connotations—for an event dreamed up by the Union Pacific. Frontier Days was the brainchild of Frederick Angier, a railroad passenger agent who saw the event as a way to promote more business. Angier took the idea to Colonel E. A. Slack, editor of the Cheyenne *Daily Sun-Leader*, who endorsed the idea and called it to the attention of Cheyenne's Board of Trade, an early version of the chamber of commerce.

The very first poster advertising the September 23rd, 1897 Frontier Days announced that "a stage coach will be held up in true frontier style." In other words, Frontier Days dedicated itself neither to what was going on in 1897 nor a historically accurate portrayal of yesteryear, but capturing a western mythology—a style—of what people wanted to see.

The Cody Stampede gained steam in the 1920s, describing itself as "The Last and Best of the Old West." This festival went so far as to invent a town called "Wolfville" which permitted residents to fire pistols in the air (blanks, most of the time, anyway) and gamble with play money. A host of other Wyoming towns and cities, Casper, Jackson, Rawlins, Lusk, Pinedale, Buffalo, and Lander began

Ed Young's Orchard: The University of Wyoming and the state Board of Immigration constantly referred to Ed Young's orchard as a horticultural paradigm. Despite years of innovation and almost unbelievable hard work, Young went bankrupt and forfeited his orchard and homestead. It was sold on the Lander courthouse steps, purchased by the primary mortgage holder, the Lander State Bank, in February 1930 for $6,619.02.

cashing in on the frontier, Old West theme. Even Rock Springs, a town with a distinctly unromantic heritage of coal mining and working for the Union Pacific, held rodeos in the 1930s.

As historian Rick Ewig pointed out in his fine essay "Give Them What They Want: The Selling of Wyoming's Image between the Wars," it was during this time that Wyoming fashioned itself into a Hollywood "Old West" image. In almost all these towns, the Chamber of Commerce and civic fathers urged citizens to play the Old West part. In 1939, George Hauser, head of the Wyoming Department of Commerce and Industry, encouraged Wyomingites to wear "western garb," urging them to "give our guests what they expect."

Besides being historically inaccurate, this devotion to a romantic cowboy history obscured Wyoming's real accomplishments. The historian Gilbert Stelter noted that "Cheyenne achieved a remarkable degree of urbanity by the 1880s." It was among the first cities in the U.S. to have electric lighting. Granted, it was an experiment that produced limited success, but the progressive mode was there. Cheyenne was the showcase for the work of English architect Charles Eastlake. In 1882, an opera house opened, complete with an auditorium of carved oak and maple woodwork. It had a fifty-five by sixty-three foot stage. Lillie Langtry and Sarah Bernhardt were among the performers.

The bucking bronco image ignored, for example, people like James Cash Penny, Jr, who started his first store in Kemmerer in 1902. By 1928, when the ranching and minerals industries were on their knees, the JC Penny chain had over one thousand stores and sales of $176.7 million. Penny's secret of success was textbook pluralism. "In retailing the formula happens to be a basic liking for human beings, plus integrity, plus industry, plus the ability to see the other fellow's point of view."

Writer and beatanick Jack Kerouac, who lived on Wyoming Western mythology, attended Frontier Days in 1947. He came away deeply saddened. He saw: "Big crowds of businessmen, fat businessmen in boots and ten-gallon hats, with their hefty wives in cowgirl attire, bustled and whooped on the wooden sidewalks of old Cheyenne; farther down were the long stringy boulevard lights of new downtown Cheyenne, but the celebration was focusing on Oldtown. Blank guns went off. The saloons were crowded to the sidewalk. I was amazed and at the same time I felt it was ridiculous; in my first shot at the West I was seeing to what absurd devices it had fallen to keep its proud traditions."

Noting this passage, historian Michael Cassity said Kerouac writes this not in contempt; rather, he knew that he was a "witness to a funeral dirge for the burying of the soul of Wyoming in a very narrow grave."

VII

TWO NATIVE SONS AND THE SONG OF EXODUS

In 1957, a young master's candidate in zoology at the University of Wyoming named Tom Bell wrote his thesis, *A Study of the Economic Values of Wyoming's Wildlife Resources*. He reached a startling conclusion: In 1955, tourism and wildlife contributed $150 million to Wyoming's economy. Hunting and fishing alone produced $23 million. The same year all Wyoming crops combined—alfalfa, barley, wheat—produced about $20 million. In fact, total agricultural production in the state in 1955, including cattle and sheep, was about $100 million.

This revelation went unnoticed. It dealt with a topic unfamiliar to Wyoming: an economy unrelated to ranching and minerals, which boomed during WWII. Bell's thesis wasn't particularly complicated and employed straightforward analysis.

Not all in power were unaware of Bell's discovery. In 1953, Wyoming Stock Grower's Association president Cliff Hansen wrote, "recreation assumes more and more prominence in the scheduling of his [the average American's] life. Quite naturally the out-of-doors becomes increasingly popular in man's pattern of relaxation. The stockman today finds that he is not alone in his interest in grazing lands, as hunting and fishing increase in popularity."

In general, however, Wyoming leaders had other matters on their mind. The money, everyone knew, was not in silly things like hunting or hiking, it was in business. Big business. After WWII, Wyoming fixated on industrial growth. The target: out-of-state corporations. The theme: *Wyoming, New Frontier of Industry*. The message: come bring your business to Wyoming, we're cheap and easy. The messenger: Colonel H. C. Anderson, Secretary-Manager of the Wyoming Commerce and Industry Commission.

In 1948, Anderson put together a *Directory of Wyoming Manufacturers, Mines and Oil Producers.* The directory included an advertisement that beckoned, "Hit Paydirt in Old Wyoming."

The directory stated: "Farsighted business executives interested in the decentralization of industry, interested in the best plant sites for their business will hit paydirt in more than one way in old Wyoming."

It continued. "Here in the heart of the old West lie unbounded natural resources... deposits of iron, magnesium, bentonite, chromium, vermiculite, manganese and other important ores, rare minerals and clays and tremendous annual supplies of hides and wool. Just as important to business executives who seek locations for industry, is the abundance of cheap, widely distributed hydroelectric power; enormous coal deposits, natural gas and oil fields... transcontinental rail and airlines and thousands of miles of paved highways."

Bold print at the bottom of the page advertised what the state has long considered its ultimate advantage. "Wyoming has no state income tax on corporations or persons."

This was Schenck and his *The New Wyoming: The Land of Great Rewards* all over again, this time with an industrialized twist. The land bargains and abundance that the Office of Immigration touted were replaced with a theme of no regulations and a rugged unrestricted environment. Wyoming was the *Old West,* "decentralized," meaning few rules and regulations.

In stressing this theme, Wyoming chose to romanticize the two brief eras when rules were in short supply: the early territory, UP track-laying days (1868-1871) and the first years of statehood (1890-1893), a period when large cattlemen thought they could kill men—again, relying on outside muscle—with immunity.

More importantly, this publicity carried a strongly implied message: because we have no regulations, you can do anything you want. "Wyoming Plant Sites Will Accommodate Any Type or Size or Industry," boasted a 1948 booklet put out by the Wyoming Commerce and Industry Commission. It was "the new frontier," and, as such, was eminently exploitable.

Just as the Office of Immigration focused its attention outside the state, Wyoming's new efforts to build industry catered to non-Wyoming corporations that relied on natural resources. The state also shared Schenck's conviction that if it told the story of how much wealth lay within its counting house, industry would come. This accountant's view has persisted decade after decade. Wyoming produced, or hired consultants to produce, reports that extolled Wyoming's riches. "Wise planning may follow an exhaustive collection of unbiased facts," reported the Wyoming State Planning Board's 1st Biennial Report in 1937.

Though Schenk's efforts had gone unrewarded, corporate America did notice Wyoming in a colonial sort of way. Out-of-state-owned corporations upgraded existing trona and phosphate plants. Uranium mills sprang up around the state. Coal power plants were built in Kemmerer and Glenrock. Discoveries of bentonite and gypsum deposits led to new processing plants. US Steel Corporation started sounding serious about exploiting Atlantic City's taconite mines, which it eventually did.

A newsletter titled *Wyoming Progress Reports* heralded these events with breathless enthusiasm. Put out by a state-sponsored economic development council called the Wyoming Natural Resource Board, each issue of *Wyoming Progress Reports* carried good news: new gypsum plants; construction of a long-awaited wool factory; modernization of power plants by Pacific Power and Electric; expansion of oil refining capability; discovery of additional petroleum reserves; plans for new dams to retain Wyoming's water. In all, the numbers indicated "strong economic gains" in Wyoming.

Then came the hard part. If Wyoming had all this new activity, why weren't people staying? In 1960, Wyoming was ranked last in the union in manufacturing payroll. Traditional industries lost ground. From 1950 to 1960, farming, coal mining, and railroads lost 12,000 employees, or 11 percent of the total employment in 1950.

Agriculture in particular plummeted; farm and ranch earnings were cut in half. By 1960 their earnings represented just 2.6 percent of the state's total personal income. In 1960, the largest single source of income in Wyoming was transfer payments, much of it federal: Social Security and pension plans.

Demographers noticed a pattern in Wyoming's population. Although the overall population grew, key age groups left the state.

You Can Bet Your Boots: A 1948 promotion put out by an early economic development group, the Wyoming Commerce and Industry Commission. Wyoming is represented as the cowboy boot cornucopia of commodity wealth, an ironic interpretation of the original horn of plenty, which symbolized fertility and food, renewable and life-sustaining resources.

Starting in 1950, the National Association of Manufacturers began tracking individual states' immigration and emigration. By 1960, a painfully clear pattern emerged. Wyoming was losing people in key economic age brackets: those fourteen to nineteen, and males over thirty years of age. From 1950 to 1960, Wyoming lost 19,700 people in net migration (includes deaths and births).

In a 1965 study, University of Wyoming demographer Thomas Davis labeled this phenomenon "population leakages." Such a drain was "a severe challenge to thinly populated states where, typically, there is a scarcity of professional persons," he wrote. "The state lacks many of the amenities and jobs to retain the most productive age groups."

In a subtle plea, Thomas asked that such patterns not be buried under the carpet. "It is imperative that those who are charged with promoting the economic and social climate of an area must be aware of the subsurface developments and their relationship to the general trends," he wrote.

From 1960 to 1970, Wyoming lost 39,000 people in total net migration, despite predictions to the contrary. In 1961, Hubert J. Soher, wrote in an economic study for Pacific Power and Light, "Wyoming has virtually every requisite—except population—to become one of the greatest industrial states in the nation. It is my belief that the future rate of growth of Wyoming will equal or exceed that of other fast-growing southwestern and western states."

Soher, however, banked on commodity extraction to bring prosperity and people. Statistical data, including the 1960 Census, showed that Davis's "population leakages" were inevitable.

A 1962 report authored by the Armour Research Foundation at the Illinois Institute of Technology gave a more realistic assessment. ARF, as it was known, reached sobering conclusions about Wyoming, particularly concerning the bleak state of agriculture. On the opening page of the summary, ARF uttered the politically unthinkable: "because of its rugged mountains, barren plains and short growing season, the development of agriculture in Wyoming has historically been limited."

Barren plains. This stark phrase dramatically contradicted the official state line, which, in essence, differed little from Schenck's pamphlets. In report after report, Wyoming's Department of

Agriculture or the University of Wyoming College of Agriculture continued to claim that "agriculture has always been a major industry in Wyoming and its importance to the state's economic stability will continue."

The ARF report said that agriculture was anything but major. It was one thing for a young grad school upstart like Tom Bell to reveal possible holes in Wyoming's agricultural idyll. But it was another matter for a report paid for by the Natural Resources Board, which was heavily staffed by ranchers, to make such a direct comment. The Natural Resources Board was founded in 1951 and then headed by J. Elmer Brock, an outspoken and arch-conservative cattleman.

The report continued. "Unlike the midwestern states, where agriculture has been more concentrated, the agriculture of Wyoming has not served as a base from which a shift to a more industrialized economy could be made. The numerically limited and widely spread population resulting from this limited agricultural development has compounded the retardation of the growth of industry in several ways."

This was the "crushing handicap" that historian Lewis Gould noted about the Wyoming of 1870. But the ARF report merely took the observation to its next logical and critical step. For better or worse, most nations modernize on the backs of agriculture. By 1962, agriculture in Wyoming paid increasingly less proportionate taxes, dropping in assessed valuation from 25 percent of the total in 1950 to about 16 percent in 1960. If Wyoming had made the unlikely choice to raise taxes on agriculture, the industry could ill-afford to pay them. In 1962, the state struggled economically and it would be just five short years before Stan Hathaway discovered the state was broke.

Even if agriculture could pay, ARF discovered that Wyoming showed a propensity to, as Thomas Sowell puts it, "sterilize their own entrepreneurs." ARF found most residents (85 percent) wanted new industry. But, the report continued, "the attitude that 'Wyoming is fine the way it is', is held by key Wyoming residents who are in a position to influence industrial growth. This difference of community attitudes is to be expected, but it is unfortunate when a minority in a community can discourage growth. A minority group which does not convey an attitude of approval to a prospect, whether at the local level or on the state level, can overcome all the good done by those sincerely interested in investing their time and money in Wyoming."

At the core of this parsimony lay an unwillingness to take risks in new ideas and companies. The issue wasn't poverty alone, but a reluctance to distribute available funds, most of which were in private hands [banks]. "This appears to be attributable to the fact that the older and traditional private financial institutions are still oriented to an agricultural and cattle raising economy," said the ARF report.

Thus it was that despite a flurry of new industry, Wyoming dug itself deeper into poverty. The stark and unyielding god of numbers, however, finally made the state drop its gravedigger's shovel. In 1968, Governor Stan Hathaway discovered that Wyoming had the grand sum of $80.00 in the general fund. "That scared the hell out of me," said Hathaway. "I had to do something."

In other words, Hathaway found himself in circumstances similar to those of his predecessor, Leslie Miller, in 1932. Although a republican and of a background dissimilar to Miller's, Hathaway shared characteristics with the former governor: bluntness, formative military service (more pronounced for Hathaway), fiscal restraint, and, most importantly, the willingness to go against the grain. When the legislature met, Hathaway, raised on a homestead and bedrock conservative, suggested a 1 percent severance tax on oil, gas, and coal.

The solons responded with incredulity. Accepted wisdom said a severance tax would never pass in Wyoming. Previous efforts had little success. During the 1899 constitutional convention, a $01.5 per ton tax on coal was rejected because it would hinder an infant industry.

Governor William Ross's 1923 attempt to get corporations to "bear their fair share of taxation" inevitably sank under republican opposition. Hathaway found little had changed. "I couldn't get anybody even in my own party to introduce a bill," said Hathaway. Finally, on the last day for introducing legislation, Cliff Davis, a representative from Gillette came forward. "He said 'I'm going to introduce a bill for you, governor, because I feel sorry for you. But

I'm going to speak against it, vote against it, and it has no chance of passing.'"

The legislation initially suffered bipartisan scorn. "Such imminent politicians such as Ed Herschler (future governor), Alan Simpson (future U.S. Senator) and Warren Morton (speaker of the House) voted against it, clear on down the line," said Hathaway. "But I got it passed, because I said to those who voted against it: 'you know, if you can't buy this you better come up with something else, a plausible alternative.' They couldn't do it. So it passed."

Hathaway said he saw a boom coming, especially in coal and trona (soda ash), and wanted Wyoming to benefit. Solidly believing that Wyoming's natural resources were a ticket to economic health, Hathaway aggressively courted out-of-state corporations. He formed a team and made trips to Boston, New York, Chicago, Houston, and Florida. A 1969 economic development report said that Hathaway and sixty "goodwill ambassadors" from Wyoming visited with California industrial and financial leaders. They promoted economic development in Wyoming, hosting a series of "wild game rendezvous" dinners (including one at the Beverly Hills Hotel in Los Angeles) of moose, elk, pioneer salad, chuckwagon beans, onion gulch potatoes, Indian succotash, sourdough bread and son-of-a-gun in a sack (molasses and raisin bread pudding).

The team found a mostly receptive audience. As a twenty-year worldwide oil surplus contracted, energy corporations saw wealth in Wyoming. Hathaway's personal contacts with J. Paul Getty and Dean McGee of Kerr-McGee led to new uranium mills in Wyoming. Burlington Northern, after various meetings with the Wyoming team, constructed a railroad line in the Powder River Basin.

Critics of Hathaway's corporate courting have said such trips were unnecessary, that companies would have come regardless of personal invitations. Hathaway doesn't disagree, but insists the timing was critical. He wanted corporations firmly ensconced in Wyoming when the markets swung up.

For that reason, Hathaway felt that keeping a low-tax climate would prevent corporations from becoming gunshy. He'd been watching Montana, which had, in his opinion, "mineral riches as much as ours but they got too greedy." In other words, it taxed too heavily, another old Wyoming worry. "Perhaps there has been no more effectual plan devised, or any more widely adopted," wrote Governor John Thayer in 1875 when giving advice on how to attract manufacturing, "than that of abating of taxes, for a limited number of years, on the capital invested in such enterprises."

Wyoming discovered that world energy prices played more of a critical role in corporate decisions than any state tax policy. The 1 percent severance tax had not chased companies off. In fact, they were banging on Wyoming's door. The legislature decided in 1973 to up the ante and tack on an additional 2 percent severance tax. Hathaway balked. "We didn't need it. We had $100 million in the general fund," he said.

But the tide seemed unstoppable. "Even the oil industry was lobbying for me to put it on. They thought it was the political coup. I really hadn't planned this out, but I told them in a caucus that I'd veto the bill unless they passed a constitutional amendment that provided we can only spend the interest of the severance tax, not the corpus of the money. The next morning, Dick Jones from Cody had a bill drawn. We made a few changes then presented it to the body as a whole and, hell, it went through easily," said Hathaway.

The constitutionally protected income became the Permanent Mineral Trust Fund, which, along with an additional fund set up later, now contains a principal of over $2 billion. In fiscal year 2000, the two funds produced $118.3 million to the general fund. Hathaway revealed mixed emotions about these bulging coffee cans. While proud of the state's efforts to conserve resources, he feels they encourage a type of dependency upon the state to pay basic bills.

"I was the cause of part of that. I passed the first severance tax. I got the Permanent Mineral Trust Fund. And they've carried Wyoming's expenses very well. It bothers me that we created something that the majority of people in Wyoming said 'my god, this is a free ride.' They want more and more money going out to the local communities and schools. The truth is, we all should pay our share of governmental costs," he said.

So, does having its own *de facto* bank prevent Wyoming from assuming self-responsibility? "I hate to say this, but to some extent, yes. It wasn't intended this way. It was intended to put some money in the bank. But it was never intended to take care of everything."

In the same year that Hathaway passed the severance tax, 1969,

Tom Bell was ready to act on his own conservationist convictions. Using money he made discovering uranium, Bell started what was to become the flagship of Rocky Mountain environmental journals: *High Country News*. He badgered the Hathaway administration constantly for what he considered to be anti-environmental and exploitative public policy towards Wyoming air, soil, and water. Hathaway, in his usual forthright manner, put it plainly: "Tom Bell was on my ass for six years."

At seventy-eight, Bell's environmental conscience is unbowed. So are his goals. "I want to change the power structure in Wyoming. I'm going to get down and dirty. If it's legal or legitimate, I'll do it."

Bell is referring to what he still sees as the stockmen's continual dominance over state political affairs. "The livestock industry is the tail that wags the dog. Their influence far outweighs what they actually contribute. They're just putting it to the public. They haven't changed in philosophy since they hanged Cattle Kate and Jim Averill."

Bell spoke of the stockman's culture of complaint. It's true that sheepmen and cattle ranchers have always griped—Bell calls it "whining"—about their tough times. Recently, with the sheep industry on the verge of collapse and cattlemen year after year getting marginal prices for their product, they have reason to find times tough. In the 1970s, however, when cattle prices were high, Bell said he got an education when he covered livestock meetings for the *Riverton Ranger*.

"The cattlemen would come to a meeting about raising the grazing fee on BLM land. They'd drive up in Cadillacs or Chrysler Imperials and wearing hand-tooled cowboy boots costing $150-$200 a pair and do you know what they'd do? They'd cry the blues. They'd complain about government regulations, saying they couldn't make a nickel or they'd say they were paying too many taxes. In reality, these guys had it all. But they'd sit and complain for hours. That's their culture."

Curiously, Bell and Hathaway share similar backgrounds. Both grew up on Wyoming ranches, both were involved in dangerous flying missions in WWII, both received undergraduate degrees at the University of Wyoming, and both have dedicated their lives to serving the state. They even share a definition of what constitutes prosperity. Hathaway's view is: "paying your bills, living a life in

Howdy, and Welcome to Wyoming!

In 1965, Wyoming celebrates the 75th anniversary of her statehood. Wyoming was the 44th state to enter the Union, on July 10, 1890. In 1868, Congress had created Wyoming Territory, which was formally organized in May, 1869. The first legislature was elected in that year, and among the new laws it enacted were those which earned Wyoming its nickname of "Equality State." Women were granted not only the right to vote, but the right of guardianship over their children and the right to hold property—rights sprung from legal attitudes toward women almost unheard of in those days.

The history of the white man in Wyoming began not many years before, in 1807, when John Colter explored the region. In 1860 and 1861, the famous Pony Express made its hazardous trips before it was put out of business by the transcontinental telegraph line in October of 1861.

For a short time in the last 1860's, the heaviest population in the state was concentrated in the mountainous area around South Pass City, where Wyoming's one great gold rush was centered. Now, 100 years later, the region has become once again a great mining area, but for iron rather than gold.

Livestock and agriculture, oil and gas, and a growing tourist industry make up Wyoming's economic base. Summertime rodeos and fairs recall to the visitor the old days of cowboys and Indians in the hectic atmosphere no longer evident except in television Westerns.

The first ICBM base was established in Wyoming in 1959, and we have moved into the space age with a fine University, five community colleges, and an expanding core of industrial activity. The business climate is favorable to development; taxes are low, and transportation facilities are excellent.

There's room to grow in Wyoming, with its high altitudes and low multitudes.

Be assured of a warm welcome here; and come back often to Wonderful Wyoming!

Sincerely

CLIFFORD P. HANSEN
Governor of Wyoming

Cliff Hansen and cattle: An image taken from a 1965 book celebrating Wyoming's 75th anniversary. Here then-governor Cliff Hansen, one of Wyoming's savviest statemen, greets the reader with a healthy and wholesome cattlemen image. Wyoming, in fact, was in deep economic trouble. Three years later Hansen's successor, Stan Hathaway, discovered Wyoming only had $80 in the general fund.

which you feel that you're making some progress, and you can handle
it monetarily. There is no better place in the world to feel satisfaction than in the state of Wyoming... if you can make a good living."

Bell said that prosperity means "having enough food, transportation and maybe a few luxuries. Every day is a great and glorious
day, no matter what I have. I'm fed. I'm clothed. I'm prosperous.
Compared to others in this world, I'm rich."

The core difference between the two men appears to be one of
spiritual constitution. Hathaway has practicality written in his mar-
row; he remains unflinchingly devoted to Wyoming's rural population. Dignity to him is a good-paying job. Wyoming approved of
this ethic when he ran the state and in 1970 reelected him with a
34,000 vote majority, the largest in Wyoming gubernatorial history.

Bell is more of a mystic, a Christian who acts locally, but also at
the direction of God or Christ. He moved from his beloved Wyoming in 1974 at the suggestion of God, who told him to "pack up his
stuff and move to Oregon." He did so and stayed for nine years.
"Best thing I ever did. If I hadn't I would have ended up in Evanston
[home of Wyoming's psychiatric hospital]." When his father died,
he returned to help his ailing mother. When he drove over South
Pass and into view of Red Rim Canyon, he heard a voice say, "It's
OK for you to move back now."

Once when *High Country News* was foundering, Bell put out a
call. He told people, "if I don't get $30,000, this newspaper will go
down. Well, I got the $30,000 and paid off all my debts. We had
$30,000 in a flash. Out of the blue."

Bell eventually left *High Country News.* The newspaper moved
to Paonia, Colorado. Bell continues to worry about Wyoming and
its obsession with independence. "Independence is a two-edged
sword. You need it and it's good up to a point."

Bell admits that he was among the worst about being independent. "Wyoming is of a spirit that says independence is our God.
It's the 'just leave me alone' attitude. There are some things you
can't possibly do without help. We take things too far. The spirit of
independence is really hard to break."

Bell worries about Wyoming's superior attitude, a concern re-
lated to Jordan's worry that the state feels it has a unique history.
"That's Wyoming's myth: that we're so much better than any other

state. I wish people could see what I had in Oregon. I lived out in the sage and plains and yet I could grow peaches and walnuts in my backyard."

Bell reveres Wyoming's plains, grasslands and tremendous mountains. But he says he doesn't know if there's anything special about Wyoming "other than the feeling that this is our home, even though it looks the same as someone right across the way."

In 1970, Bell wrote in *High Country News*:

> I don't know how I would have fared in this world had I not had the great outdoors in which to roam, seek solace, heal sensitive feelings and begin to grope my way towards adulthood. I grieve that all young people cannot experience the lessons the Good Lord can teach under His blue canopy, beside some soothing brook.
>
> My lot has been cast with the simple wonders of the world. You cannot buy the light flashing from a rainbow's side in limpid waters. There is no price on the hoot of an owl from dusky woods at eventide. You can only experience a coyote by hearing his howl.
>
> My own son can experience these things. But how about my grandsons? Will the world become so crowded that they, or their grandsons, be deprived of fulfilling experiences? How can our affluent, burgeoning society continue on its way without destroying values which cannot be bought in the marketplace?
>
> I suppose it's these apprehensions which motivate my waking moments. I would have it no other way. But I wish I could assure myself, and them.

Even though written 30 years ago, Bell's concern hasn't changed. During a 1999 interview, he held out a new *Ecologist* magazine that put forth the premise that global warming is much worse than anticipated. The world, as Bell sees it, is dog eat dog. "The good Lord teaches us to forgive. The competition is like topsy [a noxious weed]. It just grew and grew."

But in 1970, both Bell's premonition of major environmental change and Hathaway's hunch of a coming boom were on the mark. Wyoming's economy was about to explode.

VIII

TSUNAMI

In October 1973, the ghosts of Schenck, Colonel Anderson, and every other promoter in Wyoming rose up and performed a celebratory jig. People finally—at long last—were going to notice Wyoming. The forces of revenge in the Middle East cast a long and favorable light over those with oil, gas, or coal in their backyard.

For those keeping tabs on the earth's energy storehouse, ample signs of change appeared before 1973. In 1970, American oil production reached 11.3 million barrels per day, a record never to be exceeded. Petroleum had been cheap. From 1948 to 1972, the average price of crude oil averaged $2.12 per barrel. Rising demand dried up surpluses that had been floating around the United States since 1957. In 1971, the Texas Railroad Commission, for the first time in 25 years, permitted 100 percent production. Oil imports to the United States nearly doubled from 1971 to 1973.

These events gave oil-producing countries financial—and political—muscle; long the self-perceived victims of colonialist powers, these nations began flexing their economic strength. On October 19th, 1973, Libya, angered by United States support of Israel in the Yom Kippur war, stopped exporting oil to the United States. Saudi Arabia followed suit.

In 1973, Wyoming ranked fifth among states in oil production, third in oil shale, seventh in natural gas, second in uranium, and first or second in coal production. Thus, roughly 100 years after rising cattle prices and good grass put Wyoming briefly on the world map, the state's natural resources would bring it back into focus.

Rarely had the maxim "luck favors the prepared" been better applied.

For roughly a century, energy companies had been prodding and snuffling under the skin of Wyoming's earth. Successful oil and coal discoveries, such as the Salt Creek Field, required pipelines and railroad tracks. Thus when energy prices catapulted through the firmament, Wyoming was ready. Like ocean tides controlled by the moon, the prices that Wyoming oil producers got for their product rose and fell dependent upon outside forces. But the Organization of Petroleum Exporting Countries (OPEC) oil embargo was a tsunami.

The political windfall was, at least at first, felt by more than out-of-state corporations. Local owners of marginal stripper wells or uranium claims suddenly found their holdings in demand. Oil service companies, drill rig owners, heavy equipment operators, miners of all sorts, housing contractors, railroad workers, and road builders all felt themselves at the center of economic attention.

For the first time in living memory, people came to Wyoming without being coaxed or lured with subsidies. From 1970 to 1980, Wyoming gained about 140,000 people; it became the seventh fastest growing state in the nation. There were jobs for all persuasions: engineers, geologists, hydrologists, accountants, lawyers, statisticians, and doctors.

It was an unexpected blessing, really. Some familiar with oil development thought Wyoming's standing as a leading producer state was waning. There hadn't been a major oil discovery (one exceeding, or having the potential to exceed, 500 million barrels) since 1906. Yet new developments in coal and natural gas fields showed production potential. The sudden prosperity made Wyoming feel good; the flood of commerce gave Wyoming financial definition. The state that prided itself in lack of restrictions wasn't about to start discriminating now. Wyoming welcomed everyone and opened the door wide.

Income to the state treasury grew from $251 million per year in 1972 to $971 million in 1980. A book needs to be written about Wyoming's 1973-1983 decade. There are so many good tales. But suffice to say that Wyoming reveled in what the outside world heard and saw. The stories of excess, of fortunes made and lost, of outrageous behavior dovetailed with Wyoming's mythological self-image, with its primitive *joie de vivre*.

Part of this was fired by Wyoming's sheer enthusiasm for commodity extraction. From statehood until the late 1960s, no one had ever said *no* to development in Wyoming; no state official on record ever turned down a federal reclamation project or told a corporation that its presence was not in the state's best interest.

For example, in 1969, the federal government and El Paso Natural Gas Company studied the possibility of using an underground nuclear explosion to unlock vast quantities of natural gas located beneath a 90,000-acre area near Pinedale, Wyoming. Governor Hathaway endorsed the project. "I'm particularly happy that Wyoming has been selected for this study which could lead to a nuclear stimulation test in a natural gas reservoir near Pinedale," he said in an official press release. There were, in fact, two such plans afoot. The Wyoming Atomic Stimulation Project (WASP), made up entirely of out-of-state corporations, was the second one. The state's history amiably accommodated everyone.

Yet hotels are not run to keep the staff company; even the nicest guest must pay the rent. In the late 1960s, Wyoming decided that its living space was undervalued. Some, like Tom Bell, wanted more discrimination than they actually got. Under the Hathaway administration, which some considered to be unhealthily pro-business, Wyoming enacted environmental legislation. Examples would be the Air Quality Act (1967), Outdoor Advertising Act (1969), Open Cut Mining Reclamation Act (1969), Land Use Act (1969), Environmental Quality Act (1973), Surface Mining Act (1973), Land Use Planning Act (1975), and the Industrial Development Information and Siting Act (1975).

The legislature debated questions new to the state, mostly "What shall we do with all this money that we have?" The tsunami did not seem so unmanageable; the marginally calmer waters permitted Wyoming to rebuild its ship as opposed to spending all its time bailing or mending ragged sails. On a practical level, legislators were inquiring: what sort of state do we want Wyoming to be? On January 16, 1976, Governor Ed Herschler asked the legislature the critical question: "What role are the citizens of this State going to play in determining the conditions under which growth and development will take place?" Herschler furthermore stated: "I would not be standing before you today if I did not believe that we in Wyoming can and must seize the initiative in determining our own future."

Then Herschler uttered the phrase for which he will be most remembered: "change will take place, but it must take place on our terms."

While Wyoming pondered its future, world commodity prices arranged to scuttle plans. In 1886 to 1887, overstocking of cattle, a worldwide glut of beef, and nasty weather had conspired to bring Wyoming's economy to its knees. The same cast of characters—outside forces and a surplus of our own resources—were at work a century later.

The first real sign of trouble came on March 18th, 1979, when a faulty feed water pump at the Three Mile Island nuclear power plant in Pennsylvania caused a near meltdown. From that moment on, the United States looked askance at nuclear power. And Wyoming, one of the nation's leading uranium producers and home to the world's largest open pit uranium mine, stood to suffer. Although there was a brief resurgence of uranium prices in the mid-1980s, the price per pound of yellowcake went from $52.45 in 1986 to $7.00 in 1994.

On December 28, 1981, the Houston-based Baker Hughes company noted that the number of rigs drilling in America for oil and gas stood at an all-time high of 4,530. Wyoming producers got $32 per barrel for their oil, and Wyoming rig count stood at a record 190. It was the apex of the energy boom. The world had enough of what Wyoming had to offer and, as the months went by, began to withdraw its financial interest. The roller coaster had reached it zenith and was about the take the state on a speedy, familiar, and breathtakingly sharp descent.

IX

THRIVING IN HARD TIMES

Wyoming newspapers of the 1980s mostly make for hard reading, a grim resumption of economic bad news. The numbers that dance around this decade are similar to those of the Great Depression. In fact, in 1986 former governor Stan Hathaway declared that was exactly what Wyoming was experiencing, "not a recession, but depression."

During the years of 1980-1990, the Census Bureau fingered Casper as the fastest-declining metropolitan area in the United States. I moved to Casper in 1982. As a writer who covered economic issues, I watched banks close, businesses collapse, ranches fold, foreclosures lock homes, and bankruptcy papers being filed by the box load. It was a front-row seat on human sorrow.

After predicting oil prices would not go below $27 per barrel, they dipped below $15 for the first time in seven years. Companies with long time affiliations in Wyoming, such as Marathon Oil, shut their doors. From 1984 to 1990, Wyoming lost forty-four banks (some due to mergers). Those remaining severely restricted their lending as loans declined by 35 percent, a decline equal to the Depression.

In 1986, Wyoming's Total Personal Income (TPI) was $6.6 billion, the lowest in the United States, a ranking it has retained ever since. By comparison, California's TPI in 1986 was $46₴ billion. From 1980 to 1990, Wyoming was the only state in the union where nonfarm personal income fell. People left in droves. By 1990, Wyoming had 458,000 people, the lowest population in the United States.

Wyoming couldn't retrench and hunker down, waiting for the

storm to blow over and just gut it out, as it did in the Depression. Nor could it turn to an undertaxed energy industry to provide financial succor, as the state did in 1968. Its citizens had seen and felt what it was like to have money. If the first level of change was recognizing the state's poverty and doing something about it, as Hathaway did in 1968, the depression of the 1980s led to a second level of examination: what did Wyoming want from the future?

Probably the culmination of this examination was the Wyoming Future's Project, a forum that asked Wyoming's residents, "Where are we, where do we want to go, and how do we want to get there?" The questions Wyoming posed were not all that different from those asked when the state boomed. But plummeting revenues added motivation to seize the initiative, as Herschler admonished, in determining Wyoming's future.

During this time, I spent nine months working with the Wyoming Future's Project. It represented to me, barely two years a resident, a serious plunging into Wyoming's world. The Future's Project hired SRI of Palo Alto, California, to write a report.

On the first page of the executive summary, SRI said, "Experience shows that economic and social progress is achieved most easily when there is a shared view concerning a problem and some degree of consensus on how to solve it." This simple statement, seemingly obvious, was to haunt the Future's Project to its end. No matter how the Project pushed for consensus, or rather pushed its participants for consensus, fundamental divides remained.

"Its ultimate solution—build from within while seeking out and filling new market niches outside its borders—couldn't be fulfilled until the state decided it wanted to build," said Linda Nix, who co-directed the Wyoming Future's Project for two years.

This attitude was not all that different from the disposition that ARF discovered in 1962, which was "the attitude that 'Wyoming is fine the way it is,'" as the ARF report stated.

The SRI report pulled no punches. Its bottom line: "Wyoming cannot continue in its old ways and still remain a good place to live."

"Wyoming is in serious economic trouble," it said, and then proceeded to hit highlights with specific details: soft energy markets for the next ten to fifteen years would give Wyoming less revenue;

the state's fragmented tourism industry needed cohesiveness; the lack of small business hurt the state; the importance of economic diversification; and a warning against providing financial assistance to companies.

Like the ARF report written twenty-three years previously, the SRI fingered agriculture as an industry in deep trouble and declared it only a minor player in the Wyoming economy, a conclusion that greatly irritated the ranching community. SRI determined that "agriculture is not responding to current public policy approaches." In bold print, SRI warned "that without a change in policy, history is likely to repeat itself—more public expenditures and less economic returns."

Eventually the Future's Project—and its not insignificant amount of work—faded away. Wyoming had money in the bank. Unlike Miller and Hathaway, Governor Mike Sullivan did not face an empty or indebted general fund, just one that faced seriously declining revenues over the next ten years. Wyoming seemed ready to gamble and it gambled in the way they knew best: attract companies with money. Not only did it want to attract businesses from the outside, but it wanted to protect—like the farmers of 1915—the few it had.

In that spirit, in 1986 the Wyoming legislature passed a bill on link-deposit loans. This permitted the state to deposit public funds in Wyoming banks which, in turn, would then loan the money to Wyoming businesses at below-market interest rates. Of a more fundamental and aggressive nature, the state's populace, after extensive lobbying by state legislators and the state treasurer, enthusiastically voted for a constitutional amendment that permitted public funds to be used as low-interest loans to manufacturers. These were called Amendment Four funds. The Economic Development and Stabilization Board oversaw both funds.

The programs did not prosper. Approximately 70 percent of the portfolio defaulted. The loan programs were, in the words of the University of Wyoming economist Shelby Gerking, "spectacular failures by any yardstick."

The money attracted few new entrepreneurs or even viable older industries that needed capital for expansion. "A later analysis of the linked deposit program revealed that it had done little to foster growth of basic business industry," wrote Gerking. "Instead it had simply become a vehicle through which business of all types (including some owned by legislators) could obtain low-cost operating funds."

More important, concluded Gerking, was that the state's fiscal structure "offered powerful incentives to simply discontinue activities that could lead to further state economic growth."

One company, however, did not go out of business. The state loaned $602,000 to UniLink, Inc., a company whose founder had two strikes against him. He was an outsider and lived in Jackson.

UniLink, in the company's own words, "develops, markets, and services accounting software." Rodger Amadon founded the company in 1983 in Jackson, where both the firm and Amadon still reside. In 1985, UniLink had fifty clients and six employees. In 2001, UniLink had fifty-five employees—none hourly. It has 27,000 software products installed at 10,000 client locations. Certified Public Accountants and CPA customers make up most of its customer base.

Amadon is the classic immigrant to the American West. He left the East seeking health and a better life. Like Theodore Roosevelt, he sought the salubrious effects of pure Rocky Mountain air. Depleted by a demanding schedule of graduate school interspersed with employment at one of New England's largest computer firms, Amadon succumbed to a truculent case of the Hong Kong flu in 1969. Rest—and reflection on his calling—demanded a change of venue. "I was soured by a year's work in the computer industry. I got out of computers because I didn't like the lack of vision. It was a money, money, money thing without much return," he said.

Relatively untraveled (he'd never been beyond Buffalo, New York, or south of Washington, D.C.) Amadon drove nonstop from New York to Jackson. He arrived in Wyoming the day after a severe blizzard. "The ride up from Rock Springs to Jackson was the most amazing eye-opening ride I ever had. When I got into Jackson, I fell in love with it, just like everybody else does, even though there was about ten feet of snow. When I got here I promised myself I'd relax and take it easy. But within three days I was working on the ski lift. The next day I got another job managing a bar at night. I was back to two jobs already."

He soon fell in love and married. Then came the classic Wyoming dilemma: how to make living? Wyoming did not allow

HIT "PAY DIRT" IN OLD WYOMING!

Farsighted business executives interested in the decentralization of industry . . . interested in the best plant sites for their business will hit pay dirt in more than one way in old Wyoming.

Here in the heart of the old West lie unbounded natural resources . . . deposits of iron, magnesium, bentonite, chromium, vermiculite, manganese and other important ores, rare minerals and clays and tremendous annual supplies of hides and wool. Just as important to business executives who seek locations for industry, is the abundance of cheap, widely distributed hydro-electric power; enormous coal deposits, natural gas and oil fields . . . transcontinental rail and airlines and thousands of miles of paved highways.

In addition to these material advantages, Wyoming offers plenty of friendliness and cooperation to new industries.

Investigate the opportunities Wyoming offers industry. Write today,

Wyoming Commerce and
Industry Commission
H. C. Anderson,
Secretary-Manager
Room 201, State Capitol
Cheyenne, Wyoming

Wyoming

NEW FRONTIER
OF INDUSTRY

WYOMING HAS NO STATE INCOME TAX ON CORPORATIONS OR PERSONS

Paydirt: Taken from a 1948 Directory of Wyoming Manufacturers, Mines and Oil Producers. The booklet included an advertisement that beckoned, 'Hit Paydirt in Old Wyoming'. The image portrays Wyoming as the epicenter of a cheap and exploitable Old West. This portrayal continues today. Current Governor Jim Geringer has declared that, 'Wyoming is open for business'.

Amadon to exercise his expertise in computers. Gritting his teeth, Amadon and his wife moved to San Mateo, California.

There, he worked as a computer specialist in a small printing firm. Two boys were born. Yet the little red schoolhouse in Wilson beckoned. "I was not going to let my kids go to school in the city. That was too much for me. When my oldest boy was ready to go to kindergarten, we moved back here in 1975. The kids loved it. We loved it. But I was still having a lot of trouble making money. Wyoming was just not ready. You couldn't make a living writing programs."

He tried. He and a local partner formed Teton Data Systems, which specialized in medical software, but the machines needed to run the programs were bulky and expensive. His partner bought him out in 1980. Again he moved, this time back to Massachusetts working for Digital Corporation. He lasted two months on the job. While still living in the East, IBM came out with the PC. This, Amadon saw, was his ticket back to Wyoming. He spent $5200 for a diskette system machine with 64K. "The day I bought it, I knew this was the answer to what I needed because it had IBM's name on it. Hardware would no longer be the problem. If I could write accounting software for that machine, I would be set."

He sold his house in Massachusetts, returned to Jackson and began writing. Working seven days a week, Amadon wrote in the loft of his master bedroom. The software muses obliged him like never before. "I had a tremendous explosion of writing ability from September to December 1982. I realized that we were really onto something. So I hired one person, Bob Kratz. He wrote the general ledger and payroll packages."

Amadon began hiring, slowly at first, but interest in the software increased rapidly. He used local CPAs for trial runs and they embraced what Amadon had to offer. Demand got serious enough for Amadon to hire more employees. Each new building never seemed big enough. They moved six times in eight years.

In 1988, UniLink won the Governor's Quality Award. In 1990, UniLink made *Inc. Magazine's* list as one of the top 500 fastest-growing software companies in the world.

Amadon reverted to classic homestead or pioneer utilitarianism. What he didn't have, he made or grew from seed. "In 1978, we donated a $15,000 computer to the high school. We weren't making any money and we really couldn't afford it. I took a full semester and taught the teachers and the students. They were all sitting out there learning, just as fast as the other. That may have been one of the neatest parts of my life."

Amadon feels his company's ability to thrive despite having technical handicaps, no usual source of qualified workers (like a university), and high living costs has only made the company stronger. In a phrase, the ability to turn adversity into opportunity remains a hallmark of UniLink. This attribute, Amadon hopes, can be applied across Wyoming, a state that clearly has this entrepreneur under its spell.

Amadon's solution is not unlike that of Wyoming native W. Edwards Deming. A man with a passion for quality, Deming turned the economy of Japan around by promoting the philosophy of self-examination. "The biggest problem that most any company in the western world faces is not its competitors nor the Japanese," Deming wrote, "the biggest problems are self-inflicted, created right at home by management that is off course in the competitive world of today." Deming furthermore believed that most problems come not from the people, but from the system. "Everyone doing their best is not the answer. Everyone is doing his best."

Amadon similarly feels that "we don't go after our own people to get things done in this state. We're spending the money outside the state pretending that other people know better than we do. And Wyoming has got a lot of very intelligent people who could get the job done."

This unwillingness to look inward worries Amadon, who feels Wyoming "has an inferiority complex." This sensation "makes [the state] feel like it's supposed to act that if they're going into the technology age and have business and prosper [then] they have to act like other states and other cities. So we wind up getting consultants from other states to see how they do it. But there's no way that they know how Wyoming operates. It's useless."

Wyoming's history of ignoring small business is not lost on Amadon. "It's not an entrepreneurship state at all. The state needs to turn within for the products and the people that it needs to function. Maybe it should say, if we can't find the means within the state, then maybe we shouldn't do it." This includes, says Amadon, the state's obsession with studies. "We have way too many studies and consultants and discussions and panels on what Wyoming needs. What we need is success by example, not by stories of what we're going to do," he said.

"I look at my 55 employees in the company. They're all wonderful people. But they don't envy me one bit. Entrepreneurship isn't created in a person. You either got it or you don't. How do you ask entrepreneurs to come to this state, when a lot of the time a person's in their entrepreneurial years and they don't even know it? They're young, they're powerful, they're doing wonderful things. Then ten years later they say, hey, you know something, I'm an entrepreneur. But you can't be an entrepreneur unless you make some money. That's known as a dreamer at that point in time. If you don't have the means to make money, then you're not going to be an entrepreneur. The state has to be willing to hire instate, hiring, encouraging, giving tax relief to encourage use of its own people. Foster a better atmosphere of money."

∞∞∞∞∞∞∞∞

Across the state, on the eastern side of the continental divide, another business owner worries about Wyoming's attitude towards small companies. Christopher McKee runs In-situ, Incorporated, a Laramie-based manufacturer of instruments used in monitoring water quality.

In many ways, McKee is an example of a local boy made good. Educated at the University of Wyoming, he took a degree in physics then went to Cornell for a master's in environmental science and engineering management. Then he returned to Wyoming.

At age thirty-four, he's not as vocal as Amadon in his concerns for Wyoming's economic troubles ("I won't comment on that," he said dryly). Instead, McKee frets about what he sees as his community's unwillingness to accommodate to new businesses. His company sits in downtown Laramie, home to the University of Wyoming.

"They don't want to create, not at least in this town, an atmosphere that would foster people coming in with a new business. We need to create an environment, beautify this town, plant more trees, for example, that would attract new businesses. What we seem to do is attract companies like a new Wal-Mart or they're talking about opening up a new mall. These aren't core businesses that will help the economy. They're mostly minimum wage [companies]. They won't make anybody rich. Of each dollar someone spends, $.50 goes out of state to corporate headquarters. It's vacuuming money out."

The 2000 Census bears out McKee's concern. Most American university towns during the 1990s boomed, especially those in the West. Gallatin County, home to Montana State University, grew by 34 percent from 1990 to 1999. During the same time, the population of Boulder County in Colorado jumped 29 percent. Cashe County, Utah, which houses Utah State University, had to deal with a 30 percent growth in population during the 1990s. Laramie, by contrast, grew at four percent.

In-situ employs seventy people, the majority of which, says McKee, are salaried. It's a transition company, a firm that started out largely dependent on mining companies for business, but then changed course. Founded in 1979 by McKee's father, Chester McKee, it made its mark as a consulting company, monitoring water quality for uranium and gold producers.

In Latin, *in situ* means "in its original place." Gold, copper, and uranium companies that run in-situ mining operations must monitor water quality assiduously. In-situ mining involves a series of injection and recovery wells. Solutions of a weak acid are pumped through the injection wells into metal-bearing ore. This dissolves the mineral at large. Then the solution, heavy with particles of gold, copper, or uranium, is drawn up through the recovery wells. Naturally, this raises concerns about contaminating underground water supplies.

"We soon realized that there was a type of instrumentation that needed to be made that would facilitate data retrieval. So we set about making equipment to do that."

"But," said McKee "we found ourselves in an awkward position of competing on consulting contracts with the very people who were using our equipment. So, we made a strategic decision to get out of the consulting business and into manufacturing."

Now, natural resource companies make up only 10 to 15

percent of In-situ's customer base. "We sell very little equipment in Wyoming. Most of our customers are in highly populated areas, east and west coast, and worldwide."

In-situ manufactures ultra-sensitive, precision data-gathering equipment that requires stringent quality control. The company does final assembly in Laramie, but contracts out their machine shop and electronic work. Very little goes to Wyoming firms. "There's no board or electronic PCBA (printed circuit board assembly) manufacturing in Laramie, or in Wyoming that we know of, so we have to go to the Front Range [of Colorado]."

McKee said they've tried working with Wyoming machine shops, but it hasn't worked out. "So, all our machine shops are on the Front Range."

Would he take more Wyoming contractors if he could? "You bet. As long as they're competitive," said McKee. Furthermore, he said he'd happily hire more Wyoming residents or UW graduates, but few qualified applicants come across his desk. For managerial and specialized engineering jobs, Mckee finds that he must once again go south to Colorado.

X

A FINE MAP FILLED WITH DETOURS

R odger Amadon and Christopher McKee are not alone in their
struggle to make a difference in an entrenched rural society.
"Entrepreneurial immigrants are moving to some rural areas, but
not to the extent that they are moving to cities," commented the Center for the Study of Rural America. "And many local entrepreneurs
are moving away, hurting entrepreneurial innovation and leadership."

Why some rural areas struggle to survive while others thrive
depends, in part, upon physical beauty of the landscape, educational levels of the populace, and demographics. Yet underlying these
reasons is an understanding that knowledge, not land, is the key to
wealth.

Once, in 1961, rocket pioneer Dr. Werner von Braun stood before a joint session of a state with a long history of rural poverty—
Alabama. He needed three million dollars to expand aerospace research at the just-budding University of Alabama at Huntsville. Alabama wasn't producing enough scientists and engineers. "Opportunity," he said, "goes where the best people go, and the best people
go where good education goes."

"Let's be honest with ourselves," he said. "It's not water or real
estate or labor or power or cheap taxes that bring industry to a state
or city. It's brainpower."

"What do you think attracted the aircraft industry to the Los
Angeles area? The desert and smog?" he asked the solons. "No, it
was UCLA and Cal Tech and the Art Institute and St. Mary's and
the University of Southern California. Unless we get—and keep—

many more bright young men and women very soon to help us carry our present load, our programs—and Alabama—will suffer."

Von Braun's message happened to concern Alabama, but it has universal application: the ultimate resource is human intellect. Since WWII, Wyoming hasn't been able to support this commodity; the young and educated drift from Wyoming like cottonwood leaves in the wind. Those who come often do not stay. From young physicians to a University of Wyoming football coach, most view Wyoming as a stepping-stone to somewhere else. To aggravate the situation, Wyoming way-of-life mythology fosters a system that favors not wealth creation, but wealth preservation. This attracts people who have made their money elsewhere and now seek a place to maintain it.

Often these new immigrants buy large ranches, then lock the gates. Independently wealthy, they keep enough cattle to reap the benefits of low-rate agriculture taxation. Or they build grand homes, in which they reside six months and a day—just enough to qualify for residency—then live elsewhere. Gratefully, exceptions exist. Some transplants pour millions into Wyoming towns.

The adoptive citizens Wyoming desperately needs—young, creative, and ready to take risks elsewhere—spurn the state. Instead, they go where they have opportunity and choice. Decade after decade, immigrants and young Wyoming residents looking for a place to bloom ask themselves the same question: "How can I make a living in this wonderful state?"

At a conference held in October 1999 at the University of Wyoming titled "Leadership and the Future of Wyoming," communication major (class of 2000) Stephanie Olson came to the podium. "I don't see the opportunities for myself in Wyoming. I am looking outside."

On one level, Olson's urge to explore is typical. Each year college graduates crisscross the nation seeking work. But many will stay on native ground if they have a choice. The more Wyoming, as a matter of state policy, dwells and fusses over "old" industries—oil, gas, coal, and agriculture—the more it will remain what's commonly referred to as a colony.

Mythologist Joseph Campbell made an important distinction about mythological models: "(They) have to be appropriate to the time in which you are living." Campbell warned against confusing mythology with ideology.

For Wyoming, the mythological terms of the public-land West— *big, open, new, liberty, a fresh start*—carried definitions that could only apply during a certain period. The actual date when such meanings ceased to apply is arbitrary and in some sense unimportant. Certain national events and trends, however, forced new interpretations upon terms like *freedom* and *independence.*

The closing of public lands to homesteading, the interstate system of roads, the rise of environmentalism, to mention just a few, made public land states reevaluate their mythological vocabulary. Wyoming struggles to revise these terms into a living context. Campbell stressed that myths "do not come out of a concept system, they come from a life system."

In other words, myths have continuity. They encompass the dreams of 100 generations, but derive their power from the experience of here and now, not the experience of our forefathers. In contrast, Wyoming has allowed myths—important, affirming bigger-than-life stories—about people realizing their aspiration to grow stale and decay into ideology.

Here are six ideologies all derived from Wyoming's mythology of a wide-open state that permitted maximum freedom. They could almost be called prisons because they keep Wyoming from attending to more critical issues.

1) We could prosper if the federal government only let us.

Joseph Kalt of the Harvard [University] Project on American Indian Economic Development has interesting ideas about independence.

Now sixteen years into an on-going study of hundreds of tribes, Kalt has reached a singular conclusion: a tribe's well-being has little to do with location, natural resources, financial capital, or even education. The distinct denominator among successful tribes has been that they kicked federal officials out of decision making roles and took over their own affairs. In other words, the tribes, not the BIA, became responsible for their prosperity. Kalt said, "Actually, smart tribes haven't told the BIA to get out of the car, they've just told them to get out of the driver's seat."

Like the tribes, Wyoming has a love-hate relationship with the federal government, which owns 49 percent of the surface and 70 percent of the minerals underneath the prairie. Unlike the tribes, however, Wyoming can't elect to cast off the fetters of Washington. Occasionally, ill-fated rumblings rattle the West about the federal government transferring its land titles to respective states. Congress, however, has shown severe reluctance to give such plans, like the Sagebrush Rebellion, much credence.

So someone else controls half of Wyoming's land. The question remains: what sort of relationship does Wyoming want with Washington?

Every state suffers external pressure largely beyond its command. The federal government controls half of all Western states and 49.5 percent of Wyoming. This federal ownership has little to do with a state's prosperity. From 1991 to 1999, Wyoming's western counterparts enjoyed record job creation. Nevada, the state with the highest percentage of federally owned land, 80 percent, had the highest job growth rate in the nation. This might be considered an anomaly, but for the fact that the state with the second-highest job growth was Arizona, 43 percent federally owned, followed by Utah, 64 percent federally owned, and then Idaho, which is 64 percent federally owned.

How long, then, does Wyoming plan on blaming Washington for owning too much land? How much longer is Wyoming going to expend the energy required to fight, or look like it's fighting, the enemy instead of taking care of matters back home?

The federal government is the West's rich tenant from hell, a manic-depressive that one minute distributes aid like Christmas candy and then, depending on administrative whims, changes its mind, all the while taking offense from anyone challenging its policy. Listen to the voice of Wyoming state water engineer Clarence Johnston writing in 1910 about the boosterism promoted by the federal government in luring people to move into ceded Indian land on the Shoshone Reservation:

"The national government has been a dead weight. The opening was of the wrong kind. The lands were advertised as offering homes for all who desired to take them. The necessity of irrigation was not advertised. The plans in the process of formation by the State were not made public by the government. It was not pointed out that only by the expenditure of large sums of money could the high-lying lands be irrigated. The opening was a dismal failure. The history of the first year's progress is depressing when it is reviewed."

Two years later, another state water engineer, A. J. Parshall, lodged a complaint that could have been written today:

"Most of the people who have settled in the western states have respect for law and justice. They are accustomed to looking up to the Federal officer as persons who will see that all people are treated alike. The Reclamation Service, along with a few other Federal Bureaus, follows a policy of compelling everyone to come to their terms, regardless of their rights. If an individual succeeds in getting into court, the case is made so expensive that he cannot carry it through."

Wyoming is at the mercy of a fickle policy over which it has minimal influence. That, however, is how democratic systems typically treat a party of little pull. In 1968, at a Western Resource Conference on Public Land Policy held in Fort Collins, Colorado, Lynton Caldwell predicted that "if present demographics projections are valid, the America of the twenty-first century, and even before, will be politically dominated by the residents of great cities."

Anyone who has watched Congress the last twenty-five years can testify to the accuracy of Dr. Caldwell's prediction. Urban residents, through choices at the ballot box and support of lobbying groups, have increasingly steered federal land policy away from commodity extraction. The chances of abating or reversing such a policy to any meaningful degree appear slim. Interviewed for this book, Dr. Caldwell commented that, "While it's a guess, I tend to think there will be increasing pressure to keep public lands more or less in their natural state."

Accordingly, the longer Wyoming insists on supporting a natural resource economy, the more embittered and protracted will be its battles with the federal government.

Again, such conflicts present discouraging odds. Historically Wyoming has had its pride squashed more times than is probably good for a state. Its representatives in Washington, time and again, fight battles they stand grim chances of winning: wolf reintroduction, the formation of national parks (like Grand Teton), mining restrictions, snowmobiles in national parks, roadless areas in national forests, curbs on logging, Wilderness areas, and reductions in grazing. If they do gain the occasional battle with Washington, it is usually a short-term victory.

Most importantly, the implied message of blaming the federal government is: we can't thrive unless Washington lets us. Remember Schenck's complaint from 1912? "Irrigation, mining, lumbering and power development in this State will be practically at a standstill until a new [federal] policy is adopted."

Here's another version, this time from Governor Lester Hunt's 1942 address to the Wyoming legislature. "It has long been recognized that Wyoming will never reach full stature, that our possibilities of development and our rights as a state will never be fully attained, until the Federal Government relinquishes to the State or to our citizens individually the tremendous area of our lands now federally owned and controlled. ….Until the time when Wyoming shall become master of her own destiny, the future development, growth, prosperity, and even the happiness and contentment of our people cannot and will not reach full fruition."

Finally, a modern interpretation of the same song, circa May 2000, from the office of Wyoming Representative Barbara Cubin: "Our public lands are currently being locked away from public use by the Clinton/Gore Administration at an alarming pace. Wyoming businesses are closing their doors, other businesses are being threatened, and the responsible exploration and development of our natural resources have, for the most part, been slowed to a snail's pace."

These are the stances of a victim: someone else controls our destiny. It's the U.S. government's fault we can't prosper. The classic remedy for victimhood: stop blaming and start taking responsibility for your affairs. In one of the preeminent psychological treatises of the twentieth century, *Man's Search for Meaning,* author Viktor Frankl submitted that potential could be reached by turning "suffering into a human achievement and accomplishment."

For Wyoming, this means stop stomping its feet concerning actions over which it has little control; stop insisting on imagined plenary powers or *custom and culture* philosophies that argue that Wyoming has the right to make a living off natural resources.

Each time Wyoming ranchers argue for a below-market grazing rate on federal land, the implied message is: we can't survive without the government's help. When oil producers petition for relief due to low energy prices, the implied message is: we can't survive without the federal government. When cities and towns demand higher PILT (Payment In Lieu of Taxes, given to municipalities surrounded by untaxable federal land), the implied message is: we can't build a community without federal government money.

Such actions deepen our conviction of helplessness. If Wyoming wants less government influence, it might stop asking for federal help each time markets look shaky.

2) We cannot live peaceably with the federal government and keep our sense of honor.

All monetary exchanges, including federal appropriations, come with strings attached. The less one takes, the smaller the obligation. On general principle, it's best to accept as little outside income as possible. It's also not unwise to inquire about the costs, both financial and social, of accepting money. Wallace Farnham said that if Americans in the nineteenth century asked government to "subsidize without governing," then "western politicians raised this principle to the level of a Scriptural command."

Such trade-offs, essentially "give us the money and leave us alone", invariably end up messy. Monetary exchanges require a two-way transfer. Every benefactor wants something in return. Michael Phillips, one of the originators of Master Card, wrote in the book, *The Seven Laws of Money*, "Giving money requires some repayment; if it's not repaid, the nightmare elements enter into it."

Since ratifying the Constitution, the United States government has been in the benefactor business for states. The federal government has ample constitutional means to regulate laws critical to the day-to-day operation of each state, including, for example, aspects of communication and infrastructure. The Constitution claims both the Postal Service and postal roads as a federal prerogative.

Through the Interstate Commerce Clause, the Constitution spells out a whole series of powers the federal government enjoys over the states, a concept generally known as federalism. It's a dance of interdependence, but the federal government gets to pick the music. Dream as they might, individual states do not have the exclusive right to choreograph their own show. "States don't have rights.

States have powers. People have rights," says Clint Bolick in his book *Grass Roots Tyranny.*

Wyoming confesses to wanting limited federalism. Yet, upon examination, this appears to be a questionable claim. Could there possibly be something more meddlesome than money? Wyoming's traditional industries, oil, gas, mining, and agriculture, constantly beseech Washington for protection or more money, hence inviting government interference. They act like what's referred to in the religious realm as "cafeteria Christians"—those who pick and choose scripture in order to fit a political ideology.

Therefore, the issue is not whether or not we desire an interventionist federal government, but what *kind* of interventionist government does Wyoming want? The question to ask is not, "what sort of federal money can we tolerate?" Rather it's "what type of federal money will help us thrive? Which has the greatest cost-benefit ratio?"

For example, asking the federal government for help with installation of a fiber optic telephone line carries much less dependency than requesting the federal government to hold down, year after year, the price of grazing on BLM land. The latter request brings more polarization than relief to communities. Airline deregulation dealt Wyoming one of its severest economic blows of the last 50 years. It all but guaranteed the isolation of small Wyoming towns.

Furthermore, Wyoming understands—but discusses with great reluctance—the principle that asking for more federal money means more intervention. That old fear of being dissolved overrides any sense of sufficiency.

During the 1990s, Wyoming slowly crept up the rankings ladder of states who receive more federal money than they actually pay in taxes. As of 2001, Wyoming received $1.09 from the federal government for every dollar it paid in taxes. Still, this is considerably less than its neighbors. According to the Washington-based Tax Foundation. Montana takes $1.59 for every $1.00, North Dakota, $1.86, South Dakota, $1.46.

As long as Washington owns half of Wyoming's surface and almost three-quarters of its mineral estate, the state will receive considerable amounts of federal money. It will probably have to jump through various hoops, too. This does not mean it has surrendered a scintilla of sovereignty or relinquished any of that famously ambiguous state of being, *independence*.

3) Agriculture remains a cornerstone in the state's economy.

Wyoming espouses an agricultural philosophy without ever really being agricultural. Farmers passed Wyoming by. Plowed farmland only makes up 4 percent of Wyoming geography. At one time cattle production played an important economic role, but not now. A large-scale pastoral industry, grazing cattle and sheep, does not accommodate economic expansion well. Arid, high-elevation, grazing economies require three attributes: land, water, and political/economic protection. Economic diversity threatens all three.

In general, the higher the proportion of the populace involved in agriculture, the poorer the populace. With exceptions, societies that depend on grazing economies tend to be very poor indeed. According to the University of Wyoming's College of Agriculture, the average ranch or farm proprietor's yearly net income from 1975 to 1997 was $3,329. In 1997, the Federal poverty level for a family of four was $17,052. Granted, these numbers warrant careful comparison. A rancher's disposable income is prey to all sorts of distortions; agricultural operators can write everything under the sun off on their taxes.

For example, on a per proprietor basis, average total receipts for a Wyoming rancher or farmer in 1997 were $103,531. Yet annual production expenses for the same year, taken on a per proprietor basis, were $106,930, giving the rancher a decidedly impoverished net income of a negative $3,399. As the poet Wendell Berry commented, "The land cannot prosper unless the people using the land are prosperous."

Beginning in the 1950s, income cast a troubling shadow. The 1950 Census revealed that the median income for a Wyoming family was $3647. For a ranch family, it was about 30 percent lower, $2596. But there were other signs of change. For the first time, total oil and gas valuations equaled that of agricultural land. By 1955, oil and gas valuations surpassed agriculture land valuation. So did, for the first time in Wyoming's history, the total value of urban property.

A 1966 study by the Wyoming Employment Security Commission titled *Low Income in Wyoming* revealed the depths of Wyoming's agricultural woes. "Farmers, farm labor and farm managers were the occupations of the head of families which had the largest number of low incomes," which the report defined as annual incomes less than $3,000. The report, which analyzed 1960 U.S. Census bureau data, went through each county. It showed that, in general, the higher the proportion of residents in agriculture, the higher percentage of low incomes. Discouragingly, it found that half (52.9 percent) of the male agricultural sector in Wyoming made less than $1,500 per year.

In 1975, when beef prices reached a fifty-year-high, the only employment paying less than an agriculture job was a gas station attendant. Mining jobs, according to reports from the Employment Security Commission, paid an average of $280 per week in 1975; construction jobs $255. Even manufacturing work, which was rare, paid an average weekly salary of $212. In 1975, the average salary paid in Fremont County was $176 per week. Farm and ranch wages in the county averaged $57.

In some way, these figures tell of Wyoming's priorities. It values character above money. And when it has money, it doesn't care about showing it off. Wyoming remains one of the few states in the union with no Lexus or BMW dealership.

I recall in 1983 meeting a man at the Douglas airport who was, at the time, arguably one of the wealthiest citizens in Wyoming. John Dilts drove a dusty and dented Buick that boasted one hubcap among four tires. He wore patched jeans turned up at the cuffs and scuffed boots. The front of his crumpled felt hat was almost black from the blood of docking lambs. Then he pulled open the hangar door to reveal a nearly brand-new Bell Jet Ranger. "This," he said as casually as if he were showing off a set of lamb twins, "is just one of those things that helps a guy enjoy life."

But Mr. Dilts, as wry-humored and self-effacing as he was, received considerable income from minerals, not just from wool or lamb.

In 1998, the National Commission on Small Farms found agricultural producers nationwide to be suffering. The Commission said, "The setting of prices under near monopoly conditions allows the major processors and retailers of agricultural products to capture an increased price spread, bankrupting farmers while providing the financial ability for these agricultural industries to buy their competition, further concentrating markets and eliminating the free market on which our society depends."

The Commission concluded that the greatest thing that agriculture furnished America with was "not food or fiber, but a set of children with a work ethic and a good set of values."

Few would disagree with that.

The problem is Wyoming's way-of-life ideology insists on presenting agriculture as the exclusive vehicle for such virtues. Coal miners, railroad employees, and government workers are not, to the best of my knowledge, promoted by the state as the roots of a civil society.

Wyoming continues to advocate agriculture not as the most valuable land-use and wildlife management tool we have at our disposal, or a vitally important vehicle for keeping alive the Wyoming mythology of *the big open,* but rather as a viable way to make a living. As far as examples, one need look no further than a *Casper Star-Tribune* special advertising supplement dated March 23, 2000, dedicated to agriculture. Titled "Growing Tomorrows," it reinforces every fable, every credo needed to bolster an industry in denial.

In a governor's proclamation, Jim Geringer declared that "agriculture is one of Wyoming's top three industries and will continue to be a cornerstone of Wyoming's financial stability, with an economic impact of $1.5 billion. Cash income from Wyoming agriculture totaled about $850 million and 77 percent of farm cash receipts came from marketing livestock and livestock products."

Along with the governor's proclamations about agriculture, Ron Micheli, the director of the Wyoming Department of Agriculture, stated, "The facts are that the Wyoming tree grew strong and tall with values of hard work, honesty, courage, and unhesitating willingness to help others. And those uncompromising values that we enjoy today stem in large measure from the will, fortitude, and goodness carved out of existence on these arid, windswept high plains we call Wyoming. Since the late 1800s, ranchers and farmers faced the daunting task of surviving, transforming these high plains into a land which would produce crops and livestock that would help produce and clothe both ourselves and our growing nation."

While these figures sound impressive, what the governor and the director do not say is that in 1998 (the year of Geringer's and

Micheli's figures), the total net Wyoming farm and ranch income (after inventory adjustment) was $59.8 million.

The state furthermore perpetuates this claim of viability by stating Wyoming has 9,200 farmers and ranchers. Beef production value in Wyoming, however, outweighs production value from sheep, hogs, barley, wheat, and hay operators combined. The latter totals only 16 percent of the state's agriculture receipts. Eliminating them lops 3,700 operations off the total touted by the state. Then another culling: according to USDA figures, Wyoming has 5,500 beef operators of whom 3,300, or 60 percent, raise under 100 head of cattle. These are the true hobby ranchers.

If there is any affluence, it belongs to the 300 Wyoming ranchers out of 9,200—under 4 percent of the total—who own over 1,000 head of cattle. These tend to be the most economically viable and stand the best chance of surviving low prices. Or as the University of Wyoming's own College of Agriculture pointed out, 21 percent of Wyoming ranches produce 82 percent of the state's agricultural income. Conversely, the majority of ranches, about 80 percent, contribute little to the state financially.

All but a few states protect agriculture to some degree. So does the federal government. However, no state in the union—not even California—gives as many direct subsidies to its agricultural producers as does Wyoming. According to the Council of State Agricultural Finance Programs, thirty-five states offer some sort of financial assistance to agriculture. Most involve a form of lending using tax-exempt bonds (so called Aggie bonds) or loan guarantee programs with the Farm Service Agency as a financial partner. Only sixteen states offer direct lending to agriculture; taxpayers supply the capital for these funds. In these programs, fiscal modesty usually prevails. Montana, for example, has $3.3 million available for farm credit in 1999 and $1.6 million out on loan. The same year, Missouri allocated $1.6 million dollars of which $753,000 had been loaned out.

Wyoming, by contrast, statutorily allocated $295 million for ranch and irrigation loans, with $144 million outstanding in fiscal year 2000. These loans carry opportunity costs: lost interest that the state could have earned had it invested its money elsewhere at a higher rate of return. In 1988, the state calculated it lost $1.51 for every dollar on real estate ranch loans and $2.82 for every dollar it spent on irrigation loans.

What does it say about Wyoming that we feel obliged to subsidize ranchers so heavily? By their very nature, subsidies are a sign of fear. They make Wyoming appear as if it anticipates a black tomorrow. It's interesting to note that many of the top agricultural producing states, Nebraska, Florida, Iowa, or even mighty Texas, have no direct loan program. California's publicly funded State Water Project is paid for by the end users. Even a state like North Carolina, which had cash receipts of $7.2 billion in 1998, nine times those of Wyoming, only had $5.3 million available for direct loans.

Wyoming agricultural loan program was started when the state was near its last gasp in trying to attract farmers. Wyoming ended up not helping the small farmer and rancher, but rather the large operator. In fact, Wyoming has the largest average landholding of any state in the union, 3,761 acres.

Economies of scale have not brought prosperity. "For ranchers and farmers, success means survival," said Gerald Groenewold, president of the University of North Dakota's Energy and Environmental Research Center. "Policy makers need to be asking the question, "What is going to give your children something of value?"

Wyoming has yet to ask itself this critical question: has the state's agricultural policy left our children something of value? On a strictly monetary level, yes. Wyoming ranch real estate value in 1999 was $9 billion. But few young people seek out careers in agriculture. Henry David Thoreau saw this happening to New England in his own time. "None of the farmers' sons are willing to be farmers and apple trees are decayed," he said, "and the cellar holes are more numerous than the houses."

Yet Wyoming ranchers have left a priceless gift of open space, a legacy with profound ramifications on the state's economy and character. Aldo Leopold once observed that "conservation will ultimately boil down to rewarding the private landowner who conserves the public interest." What is the state willing to pay this 1.5 percent of Wyoming's population for keeping these lands open? This curiously remains one of most avoided questions in the state, although no one wants Wyoming's landscape to emulate Colorado's sprawling Front Range. As Colorado State University's biologist Richard Knight said,

"Non-ranching uses of land threaten or harm the land to a much greater degree than does ranching."

This question probably will not be resolved by generous subsidies. On the contrary, such incentives encourage an industry that, as a whole, struggles mightily to make a living. Conversely, it bankrolls affluent ranchers who don't need the money to survive. Wyoming cattle numbers have been climbing steadily since 1991 and now stand at levels similar to the mid-1970's, which set all-time records for cattle numbers (1.7 million). Yet average herd size has changed little, growing from 208 in 1990 to 248 in 1999.

This reflects a national trend in American agriculture. Big operators are getting bigger; the little guy is just hanging on. How much of a subsidy do these large ranchers need? "Our old affection for agriculture was a function of the enormous respect and admiration we had for the sacrifices and risks which the earlier pioneers endured," said Kim Cannon of Big Horn, an attorney with a long time interest in conservation issues. "When those sacrifices and risks decrease, and the agriculturists appear to be living about as well as everybody else (e.g. very few people are riding a horse six miles through snow to go to the one room school house), subsidies *appear* unnecessary."

Tony Malmberg, a Lander-based rancher put it this way. "I think the way to encourage resolution [of Wyoming's agricultural dilemma] is not to threaten our identity but to embrace it and help us see ourselves in a different light. If we can recognize that our forefathers were not seeking a frontier on the horizon but following a pioneer spirit in their own heart, we can build on our identity."

4) A commodity-based export economy is good for Wyoming.

As mentioned in chapter seven on Wyoming's 1970-1980s boom, the state's coffers grew wildly for a decade. While other Western states squandered their oil and gas income provided by the boom, Wyoming put 1.5 percent of its severance taxes in a trust fund, now worth $1.62 billion. In fiscal year 2000, interest from this single source produced $118.3 million, the second-largest source of revenue for the state's general fund after sales tax.

In addition the state established thirteen different funds that derive income primarily from oil, gas, and mineral leases. They're worth about $928 million and collectively earned Wyoming $68 million in fiscal year 2000. Finally, during the same year, Wyoming collected $307.2 million in royalties from federally owned oil, gas, and coal leases (producing states receive a portion, usually half, of these royalties). Throw in the $20 million that Wyoming collected from the tobacco-case settlement and you have a state that received approximately $513 million in passive revenue in fiscal year 2000.

All this derives from a natural resource economy. And what, pray tell, is wrong with receiving half a billion dollars in passive revenue from coal, oil, and gas?

First, the natural resource part of the equation. What good is all this money if it won't create opportunity for Wyoming residents? Where is the community that fosters family and continuity, a place where people have enough income to meet needs and have choices about the future? We've ended up with transient workers and a constant out-migration.

In addition, economist Jonathan Schechter found the decrease in Wyoming public school enrollment worthy of concern. "What's interesting is the breadth of this decline. Since 1991, only two counties have seen an increase in their school enrollments: Teton (sixteen percent overall growth) and Johnson (eight students in ten years, or 1 percent overall). Conversely, during the 1990s, nine of Wyoming's twenty-three counties experienced double-digit decreases in their total enrollment."

According to University of Montana economist Tom Power in his book, *Lost Landscapes and Failed Economies*, the pro-commodity theory goes something like this:

1) The environment provides a storehouse of resources waiting to be extracted.

2) These resources, and the extraction process, drive the whole economy.

3) Harvesting or mining these resources provides the only reliable source of community income.

4) Locally owned businesses rely on such extractive industries. Without them they—and the whole town—would wither.

The problem is, the quicker money comes into town, the quicker it leaves. Locally generated dollars last longer. Specific commodity development expansion, commonly called a boom, is not the same as economic development. It is rather, as Power calls it, "a prescription for dependence and instability."

Joel Kotkin, a fellow with the Davenport Institute for Public Policy at Pepperdine, observed this about grass-roots economies in his book, *The New Geography*. "[They are] even more relevant in an era when large companies are increasingly rootless and most new job creations stem from smaller, upstart firms. A quarter of a century ago, for example, Fortune 500 companies provided one out of every five private sector jobs; today that ratio is less than one in ten."

Kotkin continues, "Rather than focusing obsessively on large firms or symbolic projects like stadiums or tourist destinations, or simply seeking to cut taxes and provide financial incentives to favor large firms, communities need to emphasize those things that lead individuals and companies to remain in a particular place of their own accord."

Nations that rely on natural resource economies are among the poorest—or have the greatest disparity between rich and poor—in the world. For all its prowess in exporting natural resources, Wyoming doesn't get much in return when compared to other states in total export value. The Massachusetts Institute for Social and Economic Research, a leading number cruncher of U.S. Census data, noted that Wyoming's 2000 exports of $502 million gave it a ranking of 51st—dead last—in the nation.

5) We can rent-seek our way to prosperity.

Natural resource economies want corporations to pay the bills. Economists call this "rent-seeking," when someone else pays our debts. Wyoming is no exception; it hasn't paid its own way for years. "Wyoming revenue laws are inadequate," complained a 1932 State Board of Equalization report, "They should be modernized. At least 75 percent of her citizens pay no taxes."

Each year the District of Columbia Office of Tax and Revenue compares the tax burden for a family of four living in the largest city in each state. The 1999 study covers personal income tax; sales and use taxes; property taxes; and motor vehicle taxes that include

Gebo (above) and Jeffrey City (below): "Gebo in 1925, now is a town that has vanished from the landscape. Jeffrey City, a booming town as little as 20 years ago, is on the verge of meeting the same fate. The town went up for sale in the fall of 2001."

gasoline taxes, property taxes, and registration fees. The report shows Cheyenne ranking fiftieth out of fifty one cities for a tax burden.

Independence may be a subjective term, but it is most certainly not a pot of money given by someone else. Right now, Wyoming citizens do not, in any meaningful way, pay for the services they use. As they were in 1932, citizens are merely spectators in state government. Currently, businesses pay about 66 percent of Wyoming taxes, the highest percentage (again, other than Alaska) in the nation.

We are skilled at getting nonresidents to pay our bills. For example, energy companies do not normally absorb state severance taxes on oil, gas, and coal. They pass the cost on to the customer. Therefore, electricity users in Missouri pay the taxes Wyoming levies on its coal producers. The tax-passing phenomenon applies to outsiders who come to play. Wyoming ranks in the top ten for dependency on tourism; visitors pay about 6 percent of our state budget.

No colony has ever gained independence with someone else paying its way. How, then, do dependent nations wean themselves of largess? First and foremost is that they have a financial stake in their future. Wyoming–not Washington or energy companies–must fund its destiny. That means amending the tax code so residents start paying for more services they receive.

6) Free and independent societies neither need nor pay taxes. They don't need much in the way of services.

"People do not want social programs dismantled, they want them improved. People do not want less government, they want better government and better government will give us less government," said Governor Ed Herschler in 1976. Part of Wyoming's perennial antitax stance stems from lack of cash flow, especially from the agricultural community. Most ranchers, by necessity, live frugal and thrifty lives. This ethic of economy tends to become public policy when ranchers assume elected positions. They shun new programs or better funding because they personally have done without such improvements and therefore, so should the rest of the state.

To those who think Wyoming needs fewer services, the alternative is to undertake a self-reliance program aimed at indoctrinating Wyoming's residents to demand less from their state government.

So, then, what do we do?

We've got a good-looking road map. Wyoming concentrates on the wrong questions, however, and hence, invites ineffective if not infelicitous answers. But Wyoming can build community and have more influence over its future. Here are eight ways:

1) Move away from a fear-based economy.

Anxiety is a growth industry in Wyoming. Neither environment nor culture has created Wyoming's rendition of mythology;

it's been created by politics. The state has been told by Wyoming leaders if it doesn't dam its rivers, cut down timber, allow more grazing, drill additional oil wells and fight off the bully federal government, then it will blow away. Wyoming is a survivor. It can be more than that. It can thrive. Despite the dire portents by Cassandras, the state won't fall apart if it doesn't give tax cuts to mineral producers or subsidize agriculture.

This does not mean ignoring mining, oil, and gas. Wyoming climbed out of the poorhouse on mineral revenue. It will continue to play a significant role in Wyoming's economy. However, states or nations that do not use commodity wealth primarily as a stepping-stone to a manufacturing or service sector economy face continual struggle to pay bills. Furthermore, because outside forces drive natural resource prices, focusing on them diverts Wyoming from building an economy from inside the state.

Wyoming continues to be fixated on potential. *This place has such great possibilities* is the recurring theme. But something always has to happen before the dreams can materialize: we need irrigation water; we need rain; we need more bottomland; we need permits; we need a less overbearing federal presence; we need additional capital. These are all demands usually dependent on outside powers or authorities. This is a setup for guaranteed disappointment, another model of the feudal system with master and servant. Take stock in the here and now. Concentrate on what Wyoming has.

2) Take active steps to reinvigorate our mythology of freedom.

Freedom in Wyoming won't disappear if the nineteenth century version (I have the *liberty* to do whatever I want) is tucked away in the closet. Leave Patrick Henry heroics to Hollywood and tourist commissions.

If Wyoming wants to staunch its diaspora, we need to encourage Wyoming's creative minds, both young and old, to think: "It's OK to be different, or it's OK to think like an individual—to be able to keep *inner* independence—in the face of a complicated society that constantly demands trade-offs." The classic settle-the-West mythology leaves no shade of gray. Strong men don't compromise. Owen Wister's Virginian was virtuous and Trampas an evil bastard. Plain as pie. Yet as historian Richard White pointed out, "Wister's cowboys got drunk, frequented prostitutes, gambled, slept with other men's wives, and killed each other, but their life and violence was, nonetheless, 'pure.'"

For example, what is a Wyoming kid supposed to think about his or her future when the only license plate available is one with a cowboy on it? If someone wants to buy into the Western image, fine, keep the plate in perpetuity. Let Stub holding onto Steamboat be among the four or five motifs the state offers. A state manifests its mythology in the choices it makes, including something as simple as picking a license plate.

The limited vision offered to youth tends to form a shallow confidence to one's future. Scott Farris worked for years in Wyoming's public arena. Bureau chief for UPI, speechwriter for senators, governors and a congressional candidate himself, Farris's last job was legislative liaison to the University of Wyoming. He regularly fielded job offers from outside the state, but refused to leave Wyoming until health issues required that he live at a lower altitude.

When working at the University of Wyoming, he noticed that the "first thing UW graduates ask themselves is, 'who am I going to go work for?' rather than 'I'd like to do—you fill in the blank—but I don't see any of that [kind of business] in Wyoming, so I should go start one.' There's a real lack of confidence that you can create a business and be successful at it. They don't see the same opportunity that our forefathers saw."

Farris thinks the problem lies in role models. "Let's overhaul our role models to include small businesses in Wyoming mythology. Those guys are always relegated to the shadows. When we think of business, the only concept we have is multinational corporations that come here and give us jobs. And they are, parenthetically, the companies who are consolidating and losing employees."

Ann Kreilkamp of Jackson cofounded and currently edits the on-line *Crone Chronicles, a Journal of Conscious Aging.* She concurs with Farris. She feels Wyoming is "not educating people to be entrepreneurial."

Being entrepreneurial, in Krielkamp's mind, does not include the ability to find a job. "It does not mean looking to the outside world to provide for you. It's 'Who am I? What are my gifts and how do I give [them] to the world?' People are always 'looking for a job.' That strikes me as strange. To me, that's victim consciousness."

"You'd think with all this space available for possibilities, there'd be risk-taking here. What keeps people down? Then you go around in these little towns and see how many of them have satellite dishes. They're looking at someone else's picture."

That picture thankfully is changing. In October 1999, the University of Wyoming, in cooperation with the Wyoming Business Council, founded the Research Products Center. In 2000, it sponsored an Entrepreneurship Competition offering a $10,000 prize for the best business plan from a University of Wyoming student. Three graduate students who designed a piece of rock-climbing equipment, a composite carabiner, took first place.

3) Stop promoting Hollywood history.

The German film maker Ernst Lubitsch once commented, "There is Paramount Paris and Metro Paris, and of course the real Paris. Paramount's is the most Parisian of all."

Currently Wyoming projects a Paramount Wyoming image. It is not doing much for creating abundance. Scott Farris put it this way: "History matters. You can't promote a [historical] image that's patently false and expect that good things are going to happen. If the only thing you talk about is a select part of our heritage, then we're stuck. The only thing we celebrate in Wyoming is agriculture, extractive stuff, and natural resources."

Wyoming's Paramount history says the state has a legacy of fierce independence. Its inheritance, in fact, is largely one of passivity (it lets other people pay for services) and dependence (it has embraced energy industries and agriculture, two industries highly dependent on the federal government or price fluctuations). This translates to a salaried populace made up of government workers—county, state, and federal—railroaders, and mineral industry employees. These occupations follow the blueprints of a hierarchical workplace with a boss and a subordinate: a tough place to spark individual thinking. As one observer put it: "The economic history of Wyoming is 'working for the man.'"

There are practical solutions for maintaining a broad-based historical scope, Farris suggests, like keeping old buildings. When we don't have monuments to remind us that old mythology buckles when applied to modern times, it permits a fanciful version of history.

After the bombing of the British Parliament in WWII, Winston Churchill restored the building to its exact original dimensions, reasoning that "first we shape our buildings; thereafter, they shape us," he said.

"Cheyenne had an enormously charming downtown architecture," said Farris. "In the 1950s and 1960s, Cheyenne got this idea that if buildings didn't promote the cowboy image, then they have no value. So they tear down the first Carnegie Library west of the Mississippi. They tear down this incredibly picturesque post office; they tear down the UP guesthouse, which was a magnificent structure," he said.

Not having physical reminders of the past permits us to bowdlerize our history. (Thomas Bowdler edited Shakespeare's plays in the late eighteenth century, removing passages "unfit to be read in the company of ladies.") Once you tear down a building, an historic structure, then it's much easier to write revisionist history. For example, razing the Cattlemen's Club in Cheyenne allowed us to forget the darker side of our mythology.

Fortunately, Wyoming seems to have had a recent change of heart about historic preservation. "I've nothing but good things to say about Wyoming," said John Mitterholzer of the National Trust for Historic Preservation. "There's definitely been a change in the last few years." He cites saving Sheridan's historic Sheridan Inn and Casper's successful effort to create the Nicolaysen Art Museum out of a handsome but neglected former power generating plant.

4) Inward, ho.

"History tells us that the most successful cures for poverty come from within," says economic historian David Landes. "What counts is work, thrift, honesty, patience, tenacity." These virtues Wyoming has in spades.

So, then, what needs examining is a public policy that constantly blames the outside for its troubles and, paradoxically, seeks economic salvation from external expertise or capital. This does not mean xenophobia or isolationism. We all need to holler for help sometimes. It means Wyoming is not afraid to go outside seeking new tools to accommodate its need.

This also means giving people ample opportunity to fail. As Rodger Amadon said: "The state needs to turn within for the products and the people that it needs to function." Wyoming will stumble around a bit; but defeats are integral to every success story. Building a grass-roots economy is a slow and at times painful process. It requires tolerance of error. "Perfection is not for this world; it is for some other world," said W. Edwards Deming.

5) Accept competition as a way of life.

In its fear of poverty, Wyoming shelters old industries. The very symbol of this anti-competitive mode is Wyoming's policy on grazing leases for 3.6 million acres of state lands. The procedure shuts out newcomers. Nonagricultural uses are all but excluded.

Again, this change is more symbolic than substantive. It has little to do with money, but rather represents the state keeping out new ideas or enterprise.

Wyoming has various laws that project an exclusionary image. It is a fence-out state; for example, meaning if one doesn't want black Angus munching on backyard tulips, then the homeowner, not the stockman, must erect a fence. Wyoming gives ranch owners *de facto* property rights over riverbottoms and banks, preventing any angler or boater from setting foot on land that is, in most other states, public property. The Wyoming Constitution considers waterways to be public.

6) Invest in infrastructures that foster free expression and ideas. Wealth will follow.

The state needs to fund infrastructure that keeps—and attracts—not industry but people, and not people who want to preserve wealth and live a fantasy rancher life, but creative people who want to see their dreams grow. Wealth is a natural offshoot of ideas.

Wyoming is in an unparalleled position to influence its future. Unlike the past, it now has money. Yet instead of using $513 million in mineral revenues to pay the state's bills and services, this money needs to be reinvested in infrastructure, mainly education, communication and, to some degree, transportation.

These are hardly original suggestions, but their potency remains undiminished, particularly in the age of the internet. Distance to markets assumes increasingly less importance in the success of private enterprise. Wyoming is in an ideal position to capitalize on this economy. This does not mean trying to lure Internet or information technology into Wyoming or giving state money to technology companies. It means investing in communication systems that harness the ideas of Wyoming's creative minds.

Besides laying the economic foundation for entrepreneurs, Wyoming requires institutions that foster creativity. When asked to explain Utah's economic success, then Governor Norman Bangerter reportedly said "Utah State, University of Utah, and Brigham Young University."

Wyoming is the only state in the union with just one four-year university. It's difficult to see how Wyoming will retain its more fertile minds without expanding its university system—and better funding for the one university it has. This is an area where Wyoming is unequivocally—critically—behind.

For example, the third-wealthiest university in the nation is the University of Texas (it's actually the University of Texas *system*), with about $10 billion in trust. That money initially came from oil and gas. Wyoming, for a century one of the leading energy states in the nation, has a university ranked (in 2000) 249th in assets with an endowment of $141 million.

Again, the tide seems to have turned in this arena; capital campaign efforts are underway to amend this situation. As *UWYO*, the alumni publication at the University of Wyoming noted, "During the five-year period from 1996 to 2000, fund-raising totals for the UW Foundation jumped from an average of $6.5 million per year to an average of $15 million."

The depressing side of this image is that other institutions have been raising money at record rates. Despite this increase in funding the last five years, the University of Wyoming dropped in endowment rankings from 232nd to 249th. It's difficult to imagine the Wyoming legislature putting too much into its university.

7) Take the cure for Wyoming Alzheimers (we forget everything but the grudges).

"Politics is the organization of hatreds," someone once confessed. Ever since Laramie and Cheyenne fought each other in territorial times over supplying the Union Pacific, Wyoming towns and their citizens tend to be highly proprietary. "The most noteworthy fact about Wyoming's economic position, symbolized in the feuding of its towns, was the territory's backwardness relative to the rest of the Rocky Mountain west," said Lewis Gould in his, *Wyoming, A Political History.*

Subtle but potent politics of envy continue to permeate the state. When Roy Jordan was interviewing people for his *Source Book of Wyoming*, he noticed a constant anger just beneath the surface. His conclusion: "Resentment [in Wyoming] is deeper than the ice of ancient glaciers. State officials have a deep-seated resentment of the government and their bureaucratic bosses. They'd say things off-hand like, 'the legislature has no respect for this department' or 'I'm sure as hell not going to vote this year' or 'we don't like them and they don't like us.'"

While Wyoming has an egalitarian working-class background, it also is a state where few have much, mostly land. Wyoming has the largest average landholding of any state, 3,791 acres, according to the USDA. This creates a fundamental rift between homesteader ideology and reality. Wyoming doesn't have many small independent ranches, although it sorely wishes it did. Small ranches are sacred: the bedrock of Jeffersonian democracy. Big ranches, however, are a symbol of persons with too much money.

This is not a modern resentment confined to Wyoming or even this country. The Roman horseman and soldier Pliny the Elder once complained that "large farms have ruined Italy." (Note that Pliny didn't just say "farms," it was "*large* farms.")

Such sentiment still lingers unaddressed in Wyoming. Every once in a while it erupts, like over a proposal to give ranchers multiple hunting licenses that they, in turn, could sell to any hunter. With Old Testament fury, resident hunters lashed out at the proposal, demonizing Those Rich Bastards, those billionaires with all that land. Hurling terms like "land barons pocketing the profits" and "wealthy out-of-state ranchers," hunters showed up by the hundreds at public meetings.

Another example of the politics of envy is the state's relationship to the Jackson Hole Valley, Wyoming's only ultra-wealthy and sometimes quirky enclave. It's the place Wyoming loves to hate.

"Jackson, that town very close to the Wyoming border," is the common sneer. Yet when we want to take a visitor to a place of great food, spectacular scenery, skiing the envy of the downhill world, hiking, or climbing, we go to Jackson. Teton County is an asset to this state, but is currently regarded as a rich, blemished conceit. It's another version of "they've got something we don't."

Wyoming needs to learn how to accept real differences and to be encouraged to ask legitimate questions without being shunned or scorned. This responsibility lies on the shoulders of Wyoming leaders. They must "have the courage to break with tradition, even to the point of exile among their peers," said Deming in his *Out of Crisis.*

8) See Wyoming as included in the center of the nation, not a century-old throwback priding itself on "Wyoming, the way the West was."
Instead of acting—and thinking—like an entity dependent on corporations and the generosity of the federal government, the state needs to embrace a pluralistic Wyo-centric attitude. Two stellar examples present themselves: geology and water.

"Wyoming is the geologic nucleus of North America," says Carol Frost of the University of Wyoming's Department of Geology. "The rest of the country formed around us."

"The modern boundaries of the state follow, more or less, what's called the Wyoming province," said Frost. "In the Precambrian terrane of the Wyoming province, there are crystals that are 4 billion years old. If you consider that the earth is about 4.6 billion years old, that puts Wyoming right in there with the other old parts of the globe. All of Colorado is a geologic afterthought."

Wyoming is the source—the fountainhead—for much of the west's most valuable resource: water. "[We occupy] a unique position among the states as a 'Mother of Waters,'" said Leslie Miller in his memoirs. Wyoming provides major tributaries for three great rivers: Columbia (Snake), Colorado (Green), and Missouri (Yellowstone). Scott Farris, who has long advocated this vision of Wyoming as a supplier of life, says this mythology makes "Wyoming not the end of the world, but at the center." This is Wyoming's great untapped, unrecognized mythology of nurture and abundance. Wyoming may be the Cowboy State, but it also provides millions in the West with a vital, life-giving source.

Charles Handy concluded his book *The Age of Paradox* with the following observation: "Change comes from small initiatives which work, initiatives which, imitated, become the fashion. We cannot wait for great visions from great people, for they are in short supply at the end of history. It is up to us to light our own small fires in the darkness."

In applying Handy's words to Wyoming, we could conclude that while the state's mythology is plug full of heroes and bigger-than-life figures, they are gone. The living, those rising each day to build a life for themselves, are now the heroes, and perhaps mighty puny ones at that, but they're the ones left to do the work.

The poet Joseph Brodsky once wrote, "the past won't fit into memory without something left over; it must have a future." In grain-growers parlance, this means we have to have carry-over from one year to the next. Wyoming can't have carry-over from something that it never had. The state's romantic past is largely fictive. It can't take this dream and shove it into the future, hoping it will someday work. Familiarity with and acceptance of the past, including actions with a less-than-heroic theme, clears the air and encourages a state to face its future with confidence, knowing that people, not dramatic heroic gestures, can solve even the gravest problems.

Wyoming needs to rediscover a long-forgotten dream, one not governed by fear, but rather by a persistent voice of self-confidence, unshaken by drought or snow in July. It permits definition, sets rules, allows exclusion without being snobbish or self-centered. A latent, fibrous core runs throughout Wyoming. People came to Wyoming to find a better life. That goal needs to be reawakened, especially in long-term residents.

Wyoming's greatest challenge is this: integrating its mythology of taking risks—and many in Wyoming did take great risks—into an economy unrelated to natural resources. It means not blaming the weather or Washington or the low population or the lack of rain on our state of affairs. It means putting your head down, opening up your heart, and taking personal responsibility for a new mythology of risk, change, and hope.

AUTHOR'S NOTES

Don't Mess With Our Myth

Page 10: Depending on whose figures you believe: A 2000 Wyoming Department of Employment study found only 42 percent of the University of Wyoming class of 1997 still working in state. A 1993 Arthur Andersen study put the figure (number of UW graduates living out of state) at between 65 and 71 percent. A University of Wyoming alumni study the same year noted that of the 52,000 alumni it keeps tabs on, 60 percent live out of state.

Unless noted, all population figures, including immigration and emigration, are derived from U.S. Census Bureau Reports. From 1990 to 2000, virtually all population growth in Wyoming came in the age bracket 34 years and older. The age group younger than 34 shrank six percent from 1990 to 2000. During the same time period, public school enrollment shrank from 100,000 to 88,000.

No governor in Wyoming's history has publicly acknowledged: See notes concerning agriculture as a ceremonial occupation (page 113).

Wyoming seems to have a mild form of what economists call "Dutch disease." The term derives from what happened when the Dutch, long a frugal merchant and trading society, discovered oil under the North Sea. Instead of helping the country, the wave of new money pushed the economy into a recession. In other words, they became poorer because they had too much money. This was not the first time this happened. Sixteenth century Portugal and Spain, awash in gold and booty from the New World, rested on their laurels. They're still trying to recover. Meanwhile, the resource-poor nations of northern Europe: Germany, Holland, England developed into innovative trading and manufacturing countries.

Page 11: Eighty dollars in the general fund: I confirmed this figure with Governor Hathaway during an interview on February 24, 2000. During the Depression, Wyoming state government largely relied on Federal money and loans, borrowed at six percent.

Dire financial straits: For example, in FY 1997, Wyoming had expenditures totaling $2.7 billion. Fortunately, the state had revenue exceeding $3 billion. However, of that revenue, $1.8 billion came from federal spending, trust fund revenue, mineral property tax, and mineral severance tax. Without this federal and mineral revenue, Wyoming would have suffered a $1.4 billion shortfall.

Wyoming is a marginal agricultural state: Statistic taken from the USDA's Economic Research Service web site.

Page 13: Perestroika: Charles Darwin's evolutionary credo applies to political systems as well as to life forms. "It is not the strongest of the species that survive, not the most intelligent," he wrote, "but ones most responsive to change."

Jordan's essay: "Wyoming: A New Centennial Reflection," found in the *Annals of Wyoming*, Volume 62, Number 3, Fall 1990 is required reading to anyone interested in Wyoming's plight.

Why in the hell should we support an institution: "The most important idea in the genesis of the land-grant college and state university was that of democracy, because it had behind it the most passionate feeling." said Allan Nevins in his book, *The Origins of the Land-grant Colleges and State Universities*. "Social and economic democracy in America means primarily liberty of action and equality of movement. Democracy implies the intellectual liberty with full freedom to move from calling to calling, rank to rank; and a mobile society, with equal freedom to move geographically, to change environment and to find without agonizing effort new positions or fields of enterprise."

Those enterprises can be far-afield from agriculture. The University of Illinois, Cornell, and the MIT were all founded as land-grant schools. Furthermore, Dartmouth, Brown, and University of North Carolina were all given land-grant status when the Land Grant College Act of 1862 was passed. Even Yale, whose concept of improving agriculture probably meant giving the garden boy a raise, was given land-grant status because it had one of the leading engineering schools in the country. It had no farm.

Imperial intolerance: This attitude from the powers at large in Wyoming has been around since territorial times. "There is a very short and swift retribution here for men who deviate from the paths of rectitude," said a Union Pacific spokesman in referring to the actions of territorial judge John Howe when he ruled against the UP in 1870. The judge was eventually removed.

Page 14: Eleven Wyoming counties: The Charture Institute, P.O. Box 4672, Jackson, Wyoming 82001, is an organization that examines issues of growth and change in places of ecological and aesthetic significance.

Ceremonial occupation: Agriculture produces about 2 percent of the state's Gross State Product. A large portion of this (71 percent) comes from the sales of calves and cattle. In 2000, agriculture contributed the smallest percentage of the state's assessed valuation of any landholder, 1.8 percent. Residential property, by contrast, paid 23 percent. Sales tax collections in Wyoming for

2000 were $413 million. Of that, agriculture paid in $1.5 million, or .03 percent of the total.

The official number for farm employment in 1999 was 12,168 (about 3 percent of the total employment), Wyoming's Economic Analysis Division does not even include agricultural employment figures in its forecast "due to its small proportion (1.5% in 1999) of total covered employment in Wyoming." The 1.5 percent is the actual number of people who are agricultural proprietors, i.e., ranchers and farmers. Depending on the year, the new money that agriculture brings into the state ranges from modest to minimal.

Like a faithful, massive draft horse hooked to a plow and wearing blinkers, Wyoming agriculture plods on, fueled by fanciful history (perpetuated, in turn, by state-generated information that borders on propaganda), hoping someday to be recognized for all its hard work. For example, report after state-generated report states that "agriculture is one of Wyoming's most important basic industries." These reports go on to define a basic industry as one that "brings new dollars into the local economy through the sale of goods and services to consumers, businesses, and institutions located outside the state."

Just how many new dollars does agricultural bring in? There are two ways to look at the numbers, a high and a low figure. Neither speaks well for agriculture. Both come from the U.S. Census Bureau "Standard Industrial Classification" or SIC categories. The low figure, referred to as the "Export Location" reported that Wyoming exports in 2000 totaled $142 million. Agricultural exports were $3.2 million, meaning agriculture contributed 2 percent to the state's basic exports.

A high export figure, usually called "Origin of Movement," puts Wyoming total exports at $502 million, with agriculture only totaling $2.3 million.

SIC figures, however, don't measure the basic value of industries very well; they deal only with goods exported out of the United States, not state to state or region to region. Agriculture exports in particular do not reveal their true value. Still, in the age of a global economy, it shows how little Wyoming agriculture contributes to Wyoming's international trade.

Wyoming Agricultural Statistician Richard Coulter further explains why he doesn't like either number. "A major problem with export statistics by state is that the exports are allocated to states based on the location of the exporter of record. So, for example, many more Wyoming ag products are exported but only after they go to another state and are co-mingled with products from other states before actually leaving the country. The original state of origin is lost in those cases. The Economic Research Service (ERS), USDA puts out a report called FATUS (Foreign Agricultural Trade of the U.S) each year. They calculate each state's value of ag exports by allocating the U.S. total value back to the states according to the proportion of the commodity that the state produced that year. So, for example, the value of cattle exports for Wyoming would be based on what percentage of all cattle in the U.S. that Wyoming produced multiplied by the total U.S. value of cattle exports. For 1999, ERS has a total value of ag exports for Wyoming of $30.5 million."

Let's use that $30.5 million figure. Then comes the key question—how much did Wyoming spend to earn a $30.5 million export? In 1999, Wyoming spent $15.2 million on its Department of Agriculture. Of that $15.2, $11.6 million came from taxes and fees from sources other than agriculture. The state loses millions each year in opportunity costs in its $295 million state farm loan program. As a 1987 University of Wyoming College of Agriculture publication stated, "all credit assistance from the government comes at a cost to society, which must be recognized regardless of whether it is direct or indirect."

A more realistic cost scenario would probably go like this:

Opportunity cost for farm loans $44.0 million
Department of Agriculture appropriation $11.6 million
Revenue lost on subsidies for State Grazing leases $ 4.5 million
Livestock Board costs $ 1.2 million

Total state expenditure $ 61.3 million

Using these figures, the state spent $61 million to earn an export of $30.5 million dollars. To tell Wyoming residents that "agriculture is one of Wyoming's most important basic industries" when, in fact, it cost the state $3_ million to earn that figure comes scarily close to propaganda. (Charts courtesy and © THE CHARTURE INSTITUTE.)

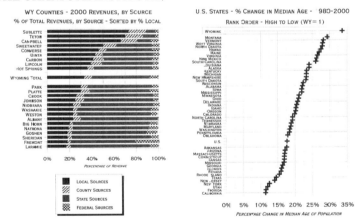

Page 16: I wanted to see if I could write a book about the west without mentioning Wallace Stegner. I obviously failed.

Page 17: Amending the Wyoming Constitution. It's filled with stern declaratives about how all money belonging to the state for public school purposes "are only to be used" for "the exclusive benefit of the schools," and that "none of such funds shall ever be invested or loaned," except for bonds issued by the county, state or federal government. Yet tacked on at the very end of the amendment are the words "or on the first mortgages on farm lands or other such securities as may be authorized by law."

Page 17: Letter, Hickok to Hopkins, Sept. 9, 1934. Lorena Hickok papers, FDR Library, Box 11.

Agriculture would have faded into obscurity: According to the Wyoming Agricultural Statistics Service, in 1932, Wyoming had almost 7,000,000 sheep (in 1999 it had one tenth of that number: 660,000). Cattle numbers in the Depression suffered a drastic drop. In 1928, only 281,000 cattle were on inventory. Between 1928 and 1935, Wyoming set state records for most acres planted of spring wheat, oats, corn, and potatoes.

Dependent of federal largess. Wyoming depends heavily on federal revenue: Almost $870 million in federal funds made up 27 percent of Wyoming's 1997 state and local revenue, the largest single source. On average, federal payments make up 19 percent of state and local revenue nationwide.

Open to opportunists of all persuasions: As T.A. Larson noted in his *History of Wyoming*, Governor Joseph Carey thought "no state had been more cursed than Wyoming by companies selling worthless stock. Capital shunned the state in consequence of many past frauds," he said.

Page 18: Bottom of the economic pile: In 2000, the US Census Bureau ranked Wyoming 48th in manufacturing dependent on exports and 48th in manufacturing employment. In 1999, the Progressive Policy Institute ranked Wyoming 50th in raising venture capital, 50th in office jobs (a point of pride for some) 48th in innovation capacity, and 50th in high tech industry. Wyoming's trump card, energy and mineral exports, looks good in volume, but not on value. The 2000 US Census ranked Wyoming 51st in total export value when compared to other states.

Almost Still Born

Page 19: Grant was not an intellectual: As civil war historian Shelby Foote said of Grant, "He had a thing that's very necessary for a great general. He had what they call 'four o'clock in the morning courage.' You could wake him up at four o'clock in the morning and tell him they had just turned his right flank and he would be as cool as a cucumber. Grant in the Wilderness, after that first night in the Wilderness, went to his tent, broke down, and cried very hard. Some of the staff members said they'd never seen a man so unstrung. Well, he didn't cry until the battle was over, and he wasn't crying when it began again the next day. It just shows you the tension that he lived with without letting it affect him... Grant, he's wonderful."

Most of my material on Grant came from John Simons's *The Complete Papers of Ulysses S. Grant*, a truly epochal work stretching 24 volumes.

Page 20: Jettison Wyoming: Wyoming, as one might imagine, howled in indignation over Grant's comments. "Wyoming to be dismembered." screeched the *Cheyenne Daily Morning Leader* on December 18th, 1872. The next day, the paper penned an editorial titled, "The Rape of Wyoming."

Advancing the cause of the Union Pacific: "Cheyenne is the creation of the Union Pacific Rail Road and by the acts of that corporation does she stand or fall." *The Cheyenne Leader*, May 9, 1868.

Page 22: There was not fertility in the soil: As it turns out, Ashford underestimated the combined forces of sweat equity and federal money; determined ranchers and irrigation projects would eventually lead water to one acre out of every thirty.

Page 25: Farmers perforce became millwrights: One of the reasons aircraft companies blossomed in Wichita, Kansas, during the 1920s was the availability of farm boys (and farmers) who were knowledgeable about machinery.

Page 26: Consternation in the voice of Governor John Hoyt: quote taken from his 1882 *Message from the Governor* speech.

Agriculture paid the highest proportion of Wyoming's assessed valuation: In order to gain a better knowledge of the state's financial history, I went through Board of Equalization annual reports, starting with the year 1891. Few sources equal these reports for documenting the rise of minerals and the decline of Wyoming agriculture. For example, Wyoming cattle alone had a value of $42 million in 1919, or 10 percent of the state's entire assessed valuation. By 1925, deflation and drought had pushed cattle values down to $12 million. Sheep values in 1925, in fact, exceeded that of cattle, with a total valuation of $14 million. Agricultural lands, however, still played the major role in providing tax revenue, provided 25 percent of the tax base. Oil, gas, and coal valuation equaled $60 million.

By 1970, cattle values were unchanged from 1919, $43 million (that's not even adjusted for inflation!) Total assessed valuation of all agricultural valuation: cattle, sheep, ranch land, improvements contributed to about 16 percent of the state's total tax base. Minerals provided 32.5 percent. In 1985, minerals provided 55 percent of the tax base; agricultural lands, 4.4 percent. The last Department of Revenue report that mentioned an assessment on cattle was 1989.

Caledonian Pitbull

Page 28: Moonlight: Most material on Moonlight came from reading his letters (and letters about him written by others, like F.E. Warren) at the Wyoming State Archives. W. Turrentine Jackson's article on *The Administration of Thomas Moonlight* in the *Annals of Wyoming*, Volume 18, July 1946, No.2 was helpful.

Vigilantism found no sympathy: Contrast this to the attitude of Amos Barber, who, as acting governor of Wyoming in 1893, knew that a group of Cheyenne cattlemen were about to administer their brand of justice in Johnson County, and did nothing to stop the activity.

Moonlight hanged two Sioux warriors up by their necks with chains, letting them choke to death: Black Kettle and Two Face had bought a white woman, a Mrs. Eubanks, from the Cheyennes. From both tribes she had experienced, as one newspaper put it, "beastly treatment." Their deaths, along with a series of preventable military gaffes, cost Moonlight his command.

Moonlight's military career in general could not be described as stellar. One hot June night in 1865, a wayward band of 1500 Sioux, Cheyenne, and Arapahoe stole seventy-four horses from Moonlight and his command, forcing the soldiers to walk ignominiously back to Fort Laramie. Moonlight was already in hot water, considering he was trying to repair a botched military order. As commander of Fort Laramie, he'd ordered only 140 soldiers to escort the Indians to Julesburg. The Indians broke away, killing some of the men. Putting himself in charge of locating the renegade Indians, Moonlight ended up not with a capture, but by the Indians stealing his horses. The press called it "Moonlight's mortification." Columnist John C. Thompson said Moonlight had "an evil genius for doing the wrong thing with the best of intent."

Page 30: The *1884 Report to the House Committee on Public Lands on the Unlawful Occupancy of the Public Lands* is a scarce commodity. The only record of this document available at the University of Wyoming remains on microfilm.

Mission Improbable

Page 34: Schenck is a man who disappeared. Frustrated by lack of material, I enlisted the help of master archivist Carl Hallberg, who, at the time, ran the Wyoming State Archives. His reply: "After jumping into the archival records in search of Roy Schenck, I soon recalled how hard it was for me to find anything about him…. He does not appear in the 1910 census for Wyoming, and is only listed in the Laramie County assessor's assessment roll for 1912 (no biographical information recorded) and in the city directory for 1913-1914."

Even so, sundry letters and Department of Immigration pamphlets provided valuable material on Schenck. The Wyoming State Board of Immigration, Biennial Reports, 1912-1923 gave a glimpse into Schenck's world.

Ignoring the event: The legislature pondered feeding the elk surplus potatoes.

Page 35: Tariffs protected the tillers of the soil and the state had friends in high places: Francis Warren, now a United States senator, had gained the presidency of the American Protective Tariff League in 1897 and presidency of the Wyoming Wool Growers Association in 1901.

He engaged in the very act he and the board professed to detest: that of exaggeration: In a way, Schenck is to be pardoned for his embellishments, for he lived in amplified advertising's golden age. The dry-farming manual of the era was Hardy Webster Campbell's optimistic *Soil Culture Techniques.* Campbell claimed that the dry West was "destined to be the last and best grain garden of the world." Probably no occupation so utilized this extravagant confidence as Western speculators and land agents.

Page 38: The Carey Act: In his 1912 report, public lands commissioner S.G. Hopkins conceded the Carey Act had fallen into dispute because of abuses in early projects—incompetent engineers, deceptive literature, lax administration.

An Awful Sense of Patience

Page 41: Parke Fox: I am grateful to Parke and Mildred Fox for sharing their stories with me. I also thank Ky Dixon, who helped me locate Parke, and set up a series of interviews.

Page 42: Grazing Homestead Act figures came from Reports to the Secretary of the Interior and Government Land Office reports. T.A. Larson gives a detailed report on the boom and subsequent failure of homesteading in pages 414–416 in his *History of Wyoming.*

Pages 44-46: A group of western historians, Wyoming's T.A. Larson among them, contributed to a data-filled series of articles on the New Deal in a 1969 issue of the *Pacific Historical Review* (vol. 38). My figures are based on their research.

Page 46: Frank Emerson: "State-of-the-state" addresses, given each year by the governor to the legislature, provided most of the quotes from this section

Page 48: General Fund overdrawn: "When I became governor of Wyoming in 1933, I inherited a $1,000,000 overdraft that had been on our books for some 20 years," Miller told the *Rawlins Times* on July 30, 1952.

Low demand caused much of oil's downfall: A January 3, 1921 *New York Times* article, *Wyoming Oil Now in Standard's Hands,* detailed Wyoming's plight.

Page 49: In 1933, cowboys and farm laborers were paid $1 per day: Wyoming Agricultural Statistic Bulletin #12, 1937.

Coal miners working at reduced wages: *Wyoming State Tribune,* 12 April 1932.

Page 51: Antitax vitriol: In 1939 Governor Nels Smith addressed the legislature. "Most people," he said, "are seeking a rest from new and troublesome regulations of their business and social lives. I am in favor of hewing governmental taxes to the bone."

Page 52: Other states incorporating the Depression era into their history: See Low's book on North Dakota, *Dust Bowl Diary,* or *Hard Times in Oklahoma,* or *Waiting On The Bounty: The Dust Bowl Diary of Mary Knackstedt Dyck.*

Invention

Page 53: The fact that the critter in Wyoming's famous image of the bucking bronco is an Indian horse buried in France is reason enough to make Wyoming reconsider this image, or at least reconsider its meaning. For a full story on Redwing, see George Ostrom's article "The Beginning of a Great Emblem," *Annals of Wyoming,* Volume 30, October 1958.

Page 55: Romantic reinvention: This mythologizing was already at work as early as 1899. "But what of the future?," queried C.G. Coutant about Wyoming. "Will the brave blood of the pioneer when assisted by the pure air of these high altitudes result in a race of men and women border on physical as well as intellectual giants?"

Two Native Sons and the Song of Exodus

Page 58: Bell's thesis wasn't particularly complicated and employed straightforward analysis: University of Montana economist Thomas Power observed, "those tools [Bell's calculations] had revolutionary implications that were being largely ignored. They asserted that there were scarce economic resources with high economic values that were noncommercial in character."

Power explains further that "from the chamber or folk economic perspective, only money flows coming in from outside the economy matter. In rural areas, natural resource-based exports are king. By focusing only on exports, Wyoming has impoverished its local economic infrastructure and all of those export dollars generate almost no economic development. In addition, it is largely the pursuit of higher quality living environments including natural amenities that is driving the 'resettlement' of the Inland West."

Page 60: Agriculture in particular plummeted: A 1970 report prepared for the Wyoming Dept. of Economic Planning and Development and University of Wyoming's College of Commerce and Industry, titled, *Wyoming: Comprehensive Economic Studies to Facilitate Development Through Planning* noted this: "Since 1950, the realized net income for the average Wyoming farm or ranch (as percentage of realized gross income) has been below the average nationally."

Page 63: For better or worse, most nations modernize on the backs of agriculture: Japan provides the most obvious example. In 1868, Japan was a poor, feudal, overwhelmingly agricultural nation with no natural resources but granite. Arable soil constituted only one-eighth of the land base. Yet by 1894, Japan had enough industrial might to defeat the Chinese in the Sino-Japanese War. Ten years later it stunned the world by beating the Russians in the Russo-Japanese War. This power came about courtesy of Japanese farmers, who paid a land tax providing a staggering 64.8 percent of Japan's annual revenue. Such a tax burden would have flattened ranchers in any state.

Page 64: Previous efforts had little success: See Henry Peterson's *The Constitutional Convention of Wyoming.*

Page 65: Perhaps there has been no more effectual plan devised: Thayer's 1875 address to the territorial legislature.

Page 67: Cattle Kate: Cattle Kate, a.k.a., Ella Watson and her husband Jim Averill, were lynched, "with no trial or bravado," as one writer put it, along the Sweetwater River on July 20, 1889. Cattlemen in the area complained that Watson and Averill were trafficking in stolen cattle. A group of local ranchers took the law into their hands and hung Watson and Averill. They were taken to trial but never convicted.

Page 69: Superior attitude: "There's nothing like it," bragged *The Cheyenne Leader* concerning Wyoming territory on November 18th, 1870. "We expect to be the recognized hub of the universe in the course of time."

Independence: Bell's comments raise a philosophical query articulated by the UCLA economist Armen Alchain. "Independent of what?" he once asked in a conversation with Montana State University economist Richard Stroup. "Markets change, and wealth rises and falls, is created and destroyed. How can anyone, or his wealth, be independent?"

Tsunami
Page 73: Critical question: Herschler's 1976 state-of-the-state speech.

How Somebody Thrived in Hard Times
Page 78: I chose to interview Amadon because he followed a Wyoming tradition of moving here and making do. When he couldn't find the employees he needed, he trained them himself, just as a small farmer or rancher tends to fabricate what he cannot afford to buy.

A Fine Map Filled With Detours
Page 85: Entrepreneurial immigrants are moving to some rural areas: This information came from an article titled *2000 Census and Growth in Rural America* put out by the Center for the Study of Rural America in October 2000.

Von Braun: Quotes taken from the Alabama House Journal, June 20th, 1961, which recorded von Braun's speech.

The legislature appropriated the money von Braun requested. Aerospace and defense industry is now a $1 billion per year industry in Alabama, according to UA-Tuscaloosa's Center for Business and Economic Research.

Page 86: Wealth Preservation: For four years running, Bloomberg's *Personal Finance* gave Wyoming an A+ (the only state to receive such a grade) in "wealth friendliness."

Leadership and the future of Wyoming: See David Broder's column on Wyoming in the Washington *Post* dated 6 October 1999 titled *A State in Trouble.*

Page 88: This has little to do with a state's prosperity: figures taken from the Bureau of Economic Analysis.

Page 90: Our public lands are currently being locked away: From a 11 May 2000 press release titled: *Cubin Opposes Bill to Increase Federal Land Ownership.*

Custom and culture: Unequivocally, *custom and culture,* the notion that local governments should have the primary voice in developing an economic policy (which typically involves honoring traditional industries, i.e. ranching, mining, and forest products) is an expedient path to poverty to all but a few. To those who find this conclusion dubious, examine the economics of *custom and culture* hotbeds, like Catron County, New Mexico or Nye County, Nevada. They are poor, especially Catron County, where 36 percent of the children live below the poverty line.

Page 91: Wallace Farnham: This quote was taken from Louis Gould's unpublished Ph.D thesis: *Willis VandeVanter in Wyoming Politics 1884-1897.*

Page 93: See Wendell Berry's essay "24 Points to Consider to Each Other," in the Sunday 9 April 2000 edition of the *Casper Star-Tribune.*

Page 95: Way to make a living: In 1998, statisticians at the Division of Economic Analysis made a rather startling observation. "Since 1986," they said, "all growth in agriculture has come from the agricultural services sector." The report further noted that almost 60 percent of those gains have come from the landscape and horticultural services sector, meaning they have "less to do with agriculture and more to do with recent gains in residential housing in Wyoming."

Here are Wyoming's leading "agricultural" producers:

Cheyenne Landscaping Inc., Cheyenne.

Cox & Fisher Inc., Powell (cattle, alfalfa, beets, employees 25, mostly seasonal beet field workers).

Hawkins & Powers Aviation, Greybull.

KE Enterprises Inc., Casper, Cheyenne.

Ken' s Landscape & Irrigation Inc., Cheyenne.

Landon' s Greenhouse & Nursery Inc., Sheridan.

Laramie Lawnery Inc., Laramie.

Oil Capital Tree Service, Casper.

Polo Ranch, Big Horn.

Pork Tech Industries, LLC, Albin (swine producer, employees about 50).

Shoshone Valley Crop & Seed Inc., Powell.

True Ranches.

Wyoming Evergreens Inc., Cheyenne, Wheatland.

Page 97: Few young people seek careers in agriculture: As Doug Cooper, himself a rancher, wrote in a March 3rd, 2001, *Casper Star-Tribune.* "The number of agricultural producers over the age of 65 have increased by 78 percent, compared to 1959, while the number of producers under age of 35 declined by 54 percent."

Thoreau. This quote comes from *The Journal of Henry Thoreau,* edited by Bradford Torrey and Francis H. Allen, Vol 3, pp. 237-238.

Leopold: From his 1934 essay *Conservation Economics.*

Correspondence with Dr. Knight dated 12 January 2001.

Page 98: Commodity-based export economy: "The key to economic development," as Nobel-winning economist Paul Samuelson said, "is not resources. The key to economic development is effective self government."

For those betting on a commodity-based economy, please look at the following graph in the 17 April 1999 *Economist* titled "Falling to Earth." (Courtesy and © 1999 *The Economist* Newspaper Limited.)

The *Economist* industrial commodity-price index, in real* $ terms
1845-1850=100

Page 100: Dead last in export value: This figure was derived using "Origin of Movement" method.

Rent seeking: Curiously, Wyoming juries are considered exemplary (or notorious, depending on your point of view) for making plaintiffs responsible for their actions. There's an unspoken credo in Wyoming that a certain accountability accompanies living and that we alone must answer to our actions. Why, then, the resistance to take responsibility for our future?

Page 108: The source for college funding comes from an annual ranking by the National Association of College and University Business Officers.

http://www.nacubo.org/accounting_finance/endowment_study/content.html

Perhaps a more fitting comparison would be the University of Nebraska Foundation. A state that began with numerous small farmers now has a land-grant university with one of the highest endowments of the plain states: $901,824,000 in 2000.

READINGS

Books and Monographs

Bell, Thomas A, *A Study of the Economic Values of Wyoming's Wildlife Resources.* Unpublished M.A. thesis, Laramie: University of Wyoming, 1957.

Bolick, Clint, *Grass Roots Tyranny: The Limits of Federalism.* Washington, DC: Cato Institute Press, 1993.

Brodsky, Joseph, *A Part of Speech.* New York: Farrar, Straus, and Giroux, 1977.

Campbell, Joseph, *The Power of Myth.* New York: Doubleday, 1988.

Clay, John, *My Life on the Range.* New York: Antiquarian Press, 1961.

Davis, Thomas S, *A Study of Wyoming People* (Demographic Series 1). Division of Business and Economic Research, Laramie: University of Wyoming 1965.

Dick, Everett, *The Lure of the Land: A Social History of the Public Lands from the Articles of Confederation to the New Deal.* Lincoln: University of Nebraska Press, 1970.

Dyck, Mary Knackstedt, *Waiting on the Bounty: the Dust Bowl Diary of Mary Knackstedt Dyck.* Iowa City: University of Iowa Press, 1999.

Flynn, Shirley, *Let's Go. Let's Show. Let's Rodeo.* Cheyenne: Wigwam Publishing Company, 1996.

Frankl, Viktor, *Man's Search for Meaning.* New York: Simon and Schuster, 1984.

Gould, Lewis, Wyoming, *A Political History, 1868-1896.* New Haven: Yale University Press, 1968.

Gould, Lewis, *Willis VandeVanter in Wyoming Politics 1884-1897.* Unpublished Ph.D dissertation, New Haven: Yale University, 1966.

Grant, Michael, *Founders of the Western World.* New York; Charles A. Scribner, 1991.

Gressley, Gene M, *Voltaire and the Cowboy: The Letters of Thurman Arnold.* Boulder: CAU Press, 1977.

Handy, Charles, *The Age of Paradox.* Boston: Harvard Business School Press, 1994.

Hassler, Paul, *Some Effects of the Great Depression on the State of Wyoming 1929-34*. Unpublished M.A. thesis, Laramie, University of Wyoming 1957.

Hendrickson, Kenneth, *Hard Times in Oklahoma; the depression years*. Oklahoma City: Oklahoma Historical Society, 1983.

Jordan, Roy, Wyoming, *A Source Book*. Boulder: University Press of Colorado, 1996.

Kerouac, Jack, *On The Road*. New York: Viking, 1955.

Kotkin, Joel, *The New Geography; How the Digital Revolution is Reshaping the American Landscape*. New York: Random House, 2000.

Krysl, Larry, *The Effects of the Great Depression on the State of Wyoming, 1935-1940*. Unpublished M.A. thesis, Laramie, University of Wyoming, 1960.

Landes, David, *The Wealth and Poverty of Nations*. New York: W. W. Norton, 1998.

Larson, T. A, *History of Wyoming*. Lincoln: University of Nebraska Press, 1965.

Layton, Stanford, *To No Privileged Class*. Salt Lake City: Brigham Young University, Charles Redd Center for Western Studies, 1988.

Low, Ann Marie, *Dust Bowl Diary*. Lincoln: University of Nebraska Press, 1984.

Moonlight, Thomas, *Seven Vetoes*. Cheyenne: Bristol & Knabe Printing Co., 1888.

Neil, William M, *The Territorial Governor in the Rocky Mountain West, 1861-1889*. Unpublished Ph.D. dissertation, University of Chicago, 1951.

O'Brien, Edna, *Down by the River*. New York: Farrar, Straus and Giroux, 1997.

O'Neil, John, *The Paradox of Success: When Winning at Work Means Losing at Life*. New York: JP Tarcher, 1994.

Nichols, David, *Ernie's America, the Best of Ernie Pyle's 1930 Travel Dispatches*. New York: Random House, 1984.

Nye, Bill, *Forty Liars and Other Lies*. Chicago: Belford, Clarke and Company, 1882.

Osgood, Ernest, *The Day of the Cattleman*. Chicago: University of Chicago Press, 1957.

Overton, Mark, *Agricultural Revolution in England*. Cambridge: Cambridge University Press, 1996.

Peffer, Louise, E., *The Closing of the Public Domain*. Palo Alto: Stanford University Press, 1951.

Peterson, Henry J, *The Constitutional Convention of Wyoming*. Laramie: University of Wyoming, Committee on Research, 1940.

Phillips, Michael, *The Seven Laws of Money*. New York: Random House, 1974.

Pomeroy, Earl, *The Territories and the United States, 1861-1890*. Seattle: University of Washington Press, 1947.

Power, Thomas, *Lost Landscapes and Failed Economies: the search for a value of place*. Washington, D.C.: Island Press, 1996.

Roberts, Phil, *Readings in Wyoming History*. Laramie: Skyline Press, 2000.

Schenck, Roy, *The New Wyoming: The Land of Great Rewards*. Cheyenne, 1912

Roosevelt, Theodore, *An Autobiography,* New York. Charles Scribner and Son's, 1926.

Simon, John Y., *The Complete Papers of Ulysses S. Grant.* Carbondale: SIU Press, 1967.

Smith, Adam, *An Inquiry into the Wealth of Nations.* New York: Modern Library, 1937.

Sowell, Thomas, *Conquests and Cultures.* New York: Basic Books, 1998.

Stelter, Gilbert, The *Urban Frontier: A Western Case Study, Cheyenne, Wyoming 1867-1887.* Calgary: University of Alberta unpublished Ph.D. dissertation, 1968.

Stegner, Wallace, Wolf *Willow.* Lincoln: University of Nebraska Press, 1955.

Stegner, Wallace, *The American West as Living Space.* Ann Arbor: University of Michigan Press, 1987.

Torrey, Bradford, *The Journal of Henry Thoreau.* 14 Volumes, Boston: Houghton Mifflin, 1906.

Toynbee, Arnold, *A Study of History.* Oxford: Oxford University Press, 1935.

Trenholm, Virginia Cole, *Wyoming Historical Blue Book.* Cheyenne: Wyoming State Archives, 1974.

Voehl, Frank, *Deming: The Way We Knew Him.* Delray Beach: St. Lucie Press, 1995.

Walton, Mary, *Deming Management at Work.* New York: G. P. Putnam, 1990.

Wilson, David, *Ulysses S. Grant: Essays and Documents.* Carbondale, SIU Press, 1987.

White, Richard, *It's Your Own Misfortune and None of My Own: a history of the American West.* Norman: University of Oklahoma Press, 1991.

Wister, Owen, *The Virginian.* Moose, WY: Homestead Publishing, 2000.

Wyoming State Planning and Water Conservation Board, *1st Biennial report, 1935-1937.* Cheyenne.

Yergin, Daniel, *The Prize: The Epic Quest for Oil, Money and Power.* New York: Touchstone Books, 1993.

Reports, Documents, and Articles

Arthur Andersen and Company, *An Assessment of the Impact of the Economic Development Projects in Wyoming.* Atlanta: 1993.

Anderson, H. C., *You Can Bet Your Boots Wyoming's The Land of Plenty: The New Frontier of Industry.* Cheyenne: 1948.

Armour Research Foundation, *Summary of a Survey for Industrial Development of the State of Wyoming.* Chicago: Illinois Institute of Technology, 1962.

Bell, Thomas, A. *High Country News.* 28 August 1970.

Campbell, John, *Wyoming Territory, Message of Governor Campbell to the First Legislative Assembly of Wyoming Territory at Cheyenne.* Cheyenne, 1868.

Casper Star-Tribune, 1968-2000.

Cassity, Michael, "In a Narrow Grave: World War II and the subjugation of Wyoming." *Wyoming Historical Journal.* Spring 1996, Volume 68, Number 2.

Chang, Richard T, "General Grant's 1879 Visit to Japan," *Monumenta Nipponica* XXIV: 4 April 1969.

District of Columbia. *Tax Rates and Tax Burdens in the District of Columbia: A Nationwide Comparison.* Washington, DC, July 2000.

Erickson, Ken, *Pictorial Overview of the Wyoming Economy,* Prepared by the Research and Statistics Division, Department of Administration and Fiscal Control. Cheyenne, 1987.

Ferrari, David. *Wyoming 1988, A Study of Revenue and Expenditures, Volume II:* Cheyenne, 1988.

Foulke, Thomas, *et al,* "Trends in Wyoming Agriculture: Agricultural Income 1969-1997." *Wyoming Economic Atlas .*

Gerking, Shelby, "State Fiscal Structure and Economic Development Structure," *Growth and Change:* Vol. 29 (Spring 1998).

Gressley, Gene M, "Colonialism: A Western Complaint," *Pacific Northwest Quarterly 54* (1963).

Hargreaves, Mary W. M. "Dry Farming Alias Scientific Farming," *Agricultural History* 22 (January 1948).

Hayden, Ferdinand, *First Annual Report of the United States Geological Survey of the Territories, Embracing Nebraska:* (1867).

Hoyt, John, *Report to the Secretary of the Interior.* 1878.

Jackson, Terrentine, "The Administration of Thomas Moonlight," *Annals of Wyoming:* (Volume 18, Number 2, July 1946).

Johnston, Clarence, State Engineer, *Annual Report. Office of the State Engineer,* Cheyenne, 1910.

Jordan, Roy. "Wyoming: A New Centennial Reflection," *Annals of Wyoming:* (Volume 62, Number 3, Fall 1990).

Keller, Robert H, "Ulysses S Grant: Reality and Mystique in the Far West," *Journal of the* West (July 1992).

Larson, T. A., "The New Deal in Wyoming." *Pacific Historical Review* 38 (1969).

Lucas, F.E., *Wyoming State Census.* Cheyenne: Secretary of State, 1925.

Moline, Brett *et al, Impact of Agriculture on Wyoming's Economy.* Cooperative Extension Service, Dept. of Agricultural Economics, University of Wyoming College of Agriculture, 1991.

Moonlight, Thomas, "Report of the Governor of Wyoming Territory." *Annual Report of the Secretary of the Interior,* House Executive Documents, Vol. X, 50th Congress, 1st Session, Government Printing Office, Washington, 1889.

Moonlight to L.Q.C. Lamar, February 24, 1887, Executive Proceedings of the Wyoming Territory, National Archives.

Morgan, William Edward, *et al,* Wyoming: *Comprehensive economic studies to facilitate development through planning.* Prepared for the Wyoming Department of Economic Planning and Development and the Wyoming State Engineer by the Division of Business and Economic Research, College of Commerce and Industry, University of Wyoming, Laramie, 1970.

National Public Radio, Weekend Edition Sunday. *Relationship between American Society and Its Architecture* (Winston Churchill quote). Washington, D.C: 5 November 2000.

New York Times, "Wyoming Oil Now in Standard's Hands." 3 January 1921, Page 12.

Ostrom, George, "The Beginning of a Great Emblem." *Annals of Wyoming.* (Volume 30, October 1958).

Paczkowski, Andrzej, "The Storm Over The Black Book," *Wilson Quarterly.* (Spring 2001).

Parshall, A. J., *Annual Report. Office of the State Engineer.* Cheyenne; 1912.

State Board of Immigration, "Some Views of Wyoming." Cheyenne; 1908.

State Board of Immigration, "Agriculture in Wyoming." Cheyenne; 1907

Tocqueville, Alexis de, *Democracy in America.* The Cincinnati Gazette, 11 June 1860.

Turnell, Jack, "Taking the Reins." *Cow Country,* Vol.129, No. 3, 2001.

U.S. Census Bureau Reports, 1870-2000.

Wyoming Agricultural Statistics Service. *Wyoming Agricultural Statistics. 1998.*

Wyoming Commerce and Industry Commission, *Wyoming Industrial Directory.* Cheyenne, 1948

Wyoming Commerce and Industry Commission, *You Can Bet Your Boots; Wyoming's The Land of Plenty.* Cheyenne, 1948

Wyoming Department of Employment, Research and Planning & the Wyoming Department of Administration and Information, Division of Economic Analysis, *Outlook 2000: Joint Economic & Demographic Forecast to 2008.* Cheyenne, 2000.

Wyoming Employment Security Commission, *Annual Reports.* Cheyenne, 1960-1985.

Wyoming Natural Resource Board, Wyoming *Progress Reports.* Cheyenne, 1961-1969.

Wyoming State Board of Equalization, Annual Reports. 1891-1975.

Wyoming State Board of Immigration. Biennial Reports. 1912-1923.

Wyoming State Highway Commission, *10th Biennial Report.* 1934-1936.